Growth Mindset for Teens

Build Confidence, Boost Resilience, and Unlock
Your Full Potential in School and Beyond

Ben Clardy

Contents

❀ Created with Vellum

Thank You

First, thank you.

By choosing this book, you're already demonstrating something remarkable — *the courage to grow and improve.*

That's no small thing!

In fact, it's the first step toward transforming your life in profound ways that you cannot yet imagine.

But here's what makes your timing perfect:

The book your holding is part of a powerful trilogy designed specifically for ambitious young minds like yours. Each book unlocks a crucial element of future success.

 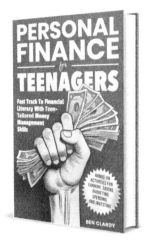 

Growth Mindset For Teens: *(This Book)* Your roadmap to unleashing your true potential by developing the mindset of champions, innovators, and high-achievers.

Practical Life Skills For Teens: Your guide to mastering the essential abilities that school doesn't teach — from effective communication to time management, from decision-making to building lasting relationships.

Personal Finance For Teens: Your blueprint for understanding wealth creation, smart money management, and building financial independence from an early age.

Think of these three books as your personal success toolkit.

While each book stands powerfully on its own, together they form something extraordinary — *a complete system for teenage success.*

For now, though, let's focus on the transformative journey ahead in these pages.

Get excited because you're about to discover how to awaken an incredible ability within yourself that most people don't even know exists.

A future of limitless potential awaits...

Introduction

Imagine this:

You stand alone in a room that's empty, aside from an old wooden table with two books lying upon it. As you approach the table, the titles of the books become clear.

The first is called: *"How To Predict The Future"*

The second: *"How To Create The Future"*

Which do you choose?

While both books provoke a sense of curiosity within you, the truth is that only one of these books holds real power — *and it's not the one that claims to predict the future...*

It's the one that shows you how to create it.

The coolest part?

You're holding that very book in your hands.

No fortune-telling, prophecies, or crystal balls — just the profound, irrefutable fact that your future isn't something waiting to be experienced — *it's something to be created.*

Most people watch life unfold passively before them, accepting whatever comes their way. But there's a group of people — *the ones who've discovered what I'm about to share with you* — who are actively designing their futures and creating their ideal lives.

The secret?

It's something called **a growth mindset.**

It's the realization that our abilities, intelligence, and talents <u>are not fixed traits</u>. They're dynamic capabilities that can be developed, expanded, and transformed in order to unlock your full potential.

Imagine shifting from feeling threatened by challenges to seeing them as stepping stones — each one bringing you closer to the life you desire. When you master this new outlook, the world changes from looking like a dangerous battlefield to something that's more like a playground of possibility!

To be clear, the goal <u>is not</u> to change who you are. The astounding truth is that <u>the power to create the future you desire is already within you</u>. It's just lying dormant — **like a sleeping giant** — waiting for you to awaken this powerful, innate ability.

The question that may come to your mind is:

> *"If everyone has this ability within them, then why don't more people use it to their advantage?"*

The answer is simple.

The path to unlocking a growth mindset is not easy. There will be discomfort. There will be moments of doubt. There will be struggle.

It's not because of these difficulties that cause most people to fail, but it's because they misunderstand the **value** of these difficulties.

To succeed where most people fail, you must understand and accept this fundamental truth:

> The struggles you'll endure are not obstacles in your path; ***<u>they are the path</u>***.

It's a great irony, isn't it? Not only is struggle completely normal, but it's also the very foundation of unlocking your growth mindset. As you'll soon understand, the magic happens in how you choose to see and react to the obstacles along your path.

Stay the path, and you'll learn how to turn:

- Fear into courage
- Doubt into confidence
- Setbacks into comebacks
- Stress into strength
- Confusion into clarity
- Problems into progress
- Obstacles into opportunities

These are the fundamental, tangible transformations that occur when you understand that life-changing growth isn't just possible — *it's inevitable* when you embrace the struggle.

So, with a world of possibilities stretching out before you, there's just one question that you need to answer:

Are you ready to awaken the sleeping giant?

Bring your curiosity, your courage, and your willingness to grow because while the path ahead won't always be easy...

...*it's <u>absolutely</u> worth it.*

Let's begin.

Chapter 1
Changing Your Mindset

"You grow through what you go through."
— Tyrese Gibson

The sound of sneakers squeaking against polished hardwood fills the gym as you stand there, heart racing. It's time for basketball tryouts. You've been counting down the days, visualizing this moment for weeks. But now that you're here, your mind betrays you with snapshots from last summer. All those missed shots in your backyard, the ball clanking off the rim again and again.

The thought creeps in before you can stop it:

"Maybe I'm just not cut out for this."

That right there? That's what psychologists call a *fixed mindset* — the silent voice whispering that your abilities are carved in stone and that past failures predict future ones. It's like wearing invisible chains that hold you back from reaching your full potential.

But here's the thing about those invisible, mental chains:

Once you learn to recognize them, *you can break them.*

Fixed Mindset vs. Growth Mindset

Picture two students both getting C's on their math tests. The first student slumps in their chair, thinking, *"This proves it — I'm just bad at math."* The second thinks, *"Okay, I guess I need to study more."*

Same class. Same grade. Two completely different takeaways.

That first student? They're stuck in a fixed mindset, believing their abilities are like concrete — once set, they never change. It's comfortable in a way because if you can't change then why even try?

The trouble with a fixed mindset is that it's a trap. It keeps you locked inside a box that you built without even knowing it. You're trapped by your own expectations, leaving little room for improvement, resilience, or discovery.

The second student? They're practicing a growth mindset. They see that C not as a reflection of their worth but as feedback — *valuable feedback* — that can be applied to get a better result next time. This mindset can transform a setback into a comeback. Maybe they'll try new study techniques, ask for help after class, or break down complex problems into smaller pieces.

For the second student, it's not just about the grade anymore; it's about the journey of becoming better. And here's the real magic: that second student isn't just learning math — they're building a toolkit of resilience and adaptability that will serve them far beyond any single test or classroom.

Mindsets Aren't Permanent

It's not as simple as being either "*Team Fixed*" or "*Team Growth.*" Instead, imagine a slider that moves back and forth depending on the situation. Maybe you have a growth mindset about sports but get stuck in fixed thinking when it comes to public speaking.

The goal isn't to flip some magical switch to *"GROWTH-MODE ACTIVATED!* Instead, the goal is to learn how to catch yourself when you're in that fixed space and gently shift your thinking into a more growth-oriented mindset.

Take Marcus, for example. Now, a seasoned chef who can coax magic out of the simplest ingredients. Ten years ago, you wouldn't have found him within ten feet of a kitchen. "*I burn water,*" he used to joke, but beneath the self-deprecating humor lay a genuine belief: cooking was something other people could do. People with natural talent. People who grew up learning family recipes. Not him. Every attempt at making dinner ended with takeout and a sink full of ruined pots.

But something shifted when his grandmother got sick. She'd always been the one to make his favorite dish – a delicious curry that filled the house with warmth and memories. Watching her health decline, Marcus faced a choice: let the recipe die with her, or push through his fear of failure.

He started small, just chopping vegetables at her kitchen table while she directed from her chair. Each weekend, he'd try one component of the dish. The onions burned the first five times. The spices were never quite right. But instead of seeing each mistake as proof that he *"just wasn't a cook,"* he started viewing them as steps toward mastery.

That curry became his gateway to a whole new relationship with cooking. Once he proved to himself that he could learn one dish, the fixed mindset began to crack — *the chains began to fall away.* He started watching cooking shows not with envy but with curiosity. Each failed recipe became a new puzzle to solve. A new challenge that brought him closer to his goal.

Today, Marcus teaches cooking classes, and he starts each session by sharing stories of his *"burning-water days."* He now recognizes, clear as day, that same old fixed mindset in his students' eyes — the belief that they're just "*not good at cooking.*" But he knows better. He's learned that culinary skill isn't some fixed trait you're born with, but a skill you gradually master, one burnt entrée at a time.

What changed for Marcus?

He shifted the way he viewed setbacks and challenges. Rather than seeing them as reasons to quit, he began using them as opportunities for improvement.

The Science Behind the Mindset

Each time you learn something new, your brain physically changes. It's what scientists call *neuroplasticity*. It creates new connections between neurons, strengthening pathways like well-worn trails in a forest. When you embrace a growth mindset, you're not just thinking differently — you're literally rewiring your brain for resilience and learning!

Dr. Carol Dweck, the researcher who first identified these mindset patterns, found something fascinating in her studies. When students learned about how their brains could grow and change, their motivation and grades improved. The simple act of understanding that improvement is possible actually makes it more likely to happen. Simply knowing that you **can** change makes it more likely that you **will** change.

If there is just one thing that you take away from this entire book, remember this:

The moment you truly understand that your abilities can grow — *that your intelligence, your talents, your capabilities aren't fixed* — you've already won! **This single realization is the key that unlocks everything else.**

Highlight it, circle it, tear this page out and pin it on your wall... whatever it takes to remember that this is the spark that lights the fire. The first domino that sets all others in motion.

Keep this in mind as we go forward.

One Word That Changes Everything

We all have that inner critic. That little, annoying voice that loves to remind us of every mistake, every awkward moment, every failure.

But what if we could teach that voice a new language?

Great news... *you can* — and it all starts with one little word:

YET.

Next time you catch yourself thinking, *"I can't,"* just add that one word to the end.

Here's how drastically it changes things...

"I can't solve these equations... ***yet.****"*

"I'm not good at public speaking... ***yet.****"*

That single word transforms dead ends into doorways.

When you say, *"I can't do this* ***yet,****"* you're telling your brain there's hope — that with effort, with time, with practice, you can and will improve.

But this isn't just feel-good philosophy. Science backs it up.

Research shows that people with growth mindsets:

- Bounce back faster from setbacks
- Take on more difficult challenges
- Learn from criticism instead of avoiding it
- Achieve more of their goals

It's like they've unlocked a cheat code for life. Not because things are easier for them, but because they see challenges from a vastly different perspective than most people. You can do the same.

"Shy Kai" and the Ripple Effect

Think of your mindset like a small stone dropped into a still pond. The ripples slowly spread outward, touching areas of your life you might not expect.

To illustrate this, let me share a story about Kai, a quiet kid who sat in the very back of his English class.

Kai started the year believing he was *"just shy."* But when we talked about a growth mindset, something clicked. He began seeing his social skills as something he could develop, rather than being a fixed trait.

The first small step forward was simple. He challenged himself to say "hey" to one new person each day. That's it. Just a simple "hey." The first few times, his voice shook, and he quickly looked away. But each small success built on the last.

After a week, he started adding "How was your weekend?" to his *"heys."* When group work came around, instead of silently nodding along, he pushed himself to ask one question about the assignment. Some days were more challenging than others — there were still moments when his heart raced before speaking up. But rather than seeing these moments as proof that he was "too shy," he began viewing them as practice rounds.

Each interaction, whether smooth or awkward, was another rep in building his social confidence. By the end of the first month, something remarkable happened: during a class discussion about The Great Gatsby, Kai raised his hand. Not just to answer a question, but to challenge another student's interpretation!

His voice was steady, his points clear. The same kid who once hid in the back row was now sparking deep classroom debates and connecting with classmates in ways he never thought possible. Not because he magically became a different person, but because he gave himself permission to grow.

Here's where Kai's story gets even more interesting:

His confidence rippled outwards.

His grades improved, not because he suddenly got smarter, but because he started asking questions when he was confused instead of hiding his uncertainty. Where once he nodded silently through confusion, he began raising his hand: "Could you explain that another way, please?" Each question felt like revealing a secret at first, but as classmates chimed in with, "I was wondering that too," Kai realized questions weren't exposing weakness — they were building strength.

When the school newspaper put out a call for new writers, something unexpected happened. Instead of immediately thinking, *"I could never,"* Kai heard a tiny voice asking, "*Why not?*" He started with small assignments — covering school assemblies and interviewing teachers he knew. By spring, he was pitching his ideas and working on feature stories. Each new challenge still brought butterflies to Kai's stomach, but he noticed something interesting... *they felt more like excitement rather than fear.*

That's the thing about mindset work. It's never just about improving one area. The improvements tend to overflow and seep into other areas. It's contagious in the best possible way!

The confidence Kai built in English class spilled into Spanish, where he stopped worrying about perfect pronunciation and started actually conversing. The shy kid from the back of English class didn't disappear — he evolved into a fuller version of himself, one who understood that discomfort wasn't a wall to hide behind, but a door to walk through.

Growth is a Lifelong Journey

A growth mindset isn't something you achieve once and check off your list. It's a practice you return to again and again. Think of it like tending a garden. You don't plant seeds once and expect them to bloom forever. You water, you weed, you adapt to the seasons. Sometimes, storms will come and damage what you've grown. But instead of seeing destruction, you start to see opportunities – chances to rebuild stronger, to try new techniques, to grow something even more beautiful than before. Every setback becomes soil for future growth.

This journey you've embarked on isn't about erasing doubt or fear. Those are innate parts of being human. Instead, it's about building a deeper trust in your ability to learn, to adapt, to rise again. Each time you choose to see a challenge as an invitation rather than a barrier, you're strengthening this trust. Each time you replace "*I can't*" with "*I can't **yet**,*" you're planting a seed for future breakthroughs.

The beauty is that it starts exactly where you are, with the very next choice you make. Maybe that's taking on a project that scares you, or returning to something you've always thought you couldn't do. Perhaps it's simply catching yourself in a moment of fixed thinking and asking, "*What if I looked at this differently?*"

These small shifts, these tiny moments of choosing growth over fear – *they add up*. Day by day, choice by choice, they build into something extraordinary: a life where challenges don't diminish you, but reveal what you're capable of becoming.

TRY IT: Create your first YET statement

Take a few minutes to catch your fixed mindset in action:

1. Think of a time that you wanted to do something, but you told yourself, *"I'm not good at that."* Write it here: _____
2. Now add *"yet"* to the end of that statement and write it again:
   _____ **...yet**.
3. What's one small step you could take this week toward changing this belief? Write it here: _____

This simple shift in language can begin to change how you think about your abilities. Post your *"yet statement"* somewhere you'll see it daily as a reminder that you're always capable of growth.

Chapter 2
Embracing Challenges

"All things are difficult before they are easy."
–Thomas Fuller

The assembly hall pulses with nervous energy. Conversations bounce off the walls, mixing with the whir and hum of dozens of science fair projects coming to life.

A robot arm extends with mechanical precision. Chemical reactions bloom in vibrant colors. And here you stand, next to your carefully crafted solar system model, wondering if you've made a terrible mistake.

Why didn't I choose something more impressive?

The judging begins in ten minutes. Your heart quickens as you imagine the questions coming your way. Every rotation of your model's planets feels slower and more clunky than before. As you make final adjustments to Saturn's rings, you notice some uncomfortable feelings within you.

That unsteady tremble in your hands?

That flutter in the pit of your stomach?

That electric tension buzzing in your mind?

Here's what most people miss in moments like these:

Despite the discomfort of these feelings, <u>they're not warning signs.</u>

Instead, these uncomfortable impulses are your brain's way of letting you know that you're in the zone where growth is actively happening.

8

The invisible zone we're talking about here *is just beyond your comfort zone,* and there are endless situations in life that will push you there, such as:

- Intimidating science fair presentations
- Math problems that seem utterly impossible
- Asking your crush to go to the movies
- Raising your hand in class when you're not 100% confident
- Sitting with a new group at lunch
- Auditioning for the school musical or play
- Starting a conversation with someone you want to be friends with
- The sports tryout that tests your limits
- Speaking up when you see someone being treated unfairly
- Sharing your art or writing with others
- Standing up to peer pressure

The potential situations are endless, but the interesting thing about it is that each time you're presented with a new challenge, you essentially only have two options for how to react:

Option #1: Retreat back into your comfort zone and stay the same

Option #2: Push beyond your comfort zone *and grow*

Why Challenges are Essential for Growth

Life has a way of continuously presenting us with obstacles. While it's natural to wish for an easier path, these challenges aren't accidents or unfortunate detours — *they're the very foundation of our personal development!*

Every time you step outside your comfort zone, you expand your understanding of what's possible.

Is it uncomfortable? *Yep!*

Will you sometimes fail? *Yep!*

When you're beyond the bounds of your comfort zone, your mind resists, and your confidence wavers. But with each unsteady step forward, you map new terrain in your capabilities.

Consider Sarah, a freshman who joined her school's debate team despite being absolutely terrified of public speaking.

Ben Clardy

Her first attempt was exactly what she feared. Her voice shook, she lost her train of thought, and she sat down feeling utterly defeated.

But she came back the following week.

And the week after that.

Each debate taught her something new. She learned to channel her nervous energy into preparation. She discovered that stumbling over words wasn't fatal — *it was just feedback about where to focus her practice.* Most importantly, she learned that confidence isn't something you wait to feel before taking action — *it's something you build through facing challenges.*

This is how *real growth* happens. Not through comfortable repetition of what you already know, but through the willingness to attempt what lies just beyond your current abilities and comfort.

Musicians don't become great by playing only the pieces they've mastered. Artists don't evolve by staying within familiar techniques. Scientists don't make breakthroughs by exploring only what's already known.

They grow by embracing *the edge of possibility.*

It's this mental shift that transforms every challenge from a threat into an opportunity for growth.

Learning to Embrace the Process

Real growth happens when we engage with challenges fully, not just endure them. Anyone can grit their teeth and push through difficulty, but the magic happens when we fully embrace these challenging moments and accept them as the opportunities that they are.

This shift in perspective changes everything.

Think about your most recent challenge. Maybe you bombed a presentation. Froze during a game. Stared at a blank page, unable to write that first sentence. That flutter in your stomach, that anxious tension in your mind? Most people interpret those feelings as warning signs. They pull back. Play it safe. Stay comfortable.

But what if these feelings weren't warnings at all?

What if they were signals pointing you toward growth?

Learn to welcome that spark of nervous energy. Chase that feeling of being right on the edge of your capabilities. The most significant moments of growth happen

10

when you're slightly uncomfortable, when the challenge feels just beyond your current reach.

The key lies in asking different questions.

Not *"Why am I so bad at this?"* but *"What could make this better?"*

Not *"When will this get easier?"* but *"What am I learning from this difficulty?"*

Not *"How can I avoid this feeling?"* but *"What opportunities does this tension reveal?"*

These questions transform challenges from threats into experiments. They convert anxiety into curiosity. They turn setbacks into data points. Most importantly, they shift your focus from judgment to growth. This isn't just positive thinking — *it's about **intentional** thinking* — the kind that produces lasting, positive growth.

Of course, the resulting transformation isn't immediate or constant. Some days, old doubts creep back in. Nervousness still appears before important moments. But now you understand these feelings differently. They're not warning signs — they're growth signals. They're not telling you to stop — they're showing you where to push forward.

Those butterflies in your stomach before a performance? *Welcome them.*

That tension before a big game? *Embrace it.*

The nervous energy before a presentation? *Let it fuel you.*

These feelings aren't your enemy. They're signals that you're alive, growing, pushing into new territory. They're the feeling of potential becoming reality.

This is where real growth lives — not in the comfortable spaces, but right at the edge of your current abilities. Learn to love that edge. Seek it out. Because that's where challenges meet opportunity, where potential meets growth, where you discover what you're truly capable of becoming.

The Power of Strategic Feedback

Every success and failure contains hidden lessons. Most people miss them entirely, seeing only the outcome.

Consider how a skilled athlete prepares for competition. They don't just practice;

- They film their performance
- They study their movements
- They analyze their decisions under pressure

Each review reveals subtle patterns: a slight hesitation before crucial plays, a tendency to rush when tired, and moments of perfect form that can be replicated. This detailed analysis transforms vague impressions into precise insights.

We all have blind spots — patterns we can't see because we're too close to them. External feedback fills these gaps in our perception. A teacher might notice that you grasp concepts intuitively but skip crucial steps in showing your work. A coach might spot tension in your form that you've never noticed. A peer might point out that your ideas are brilliant, but your explanations jump too quickly between points.

This feedback isn't criticism. It's a spotlight illuminating your path to improvement. When a music teacher points out that you speed up during complex passages, they're literally handing you the key to better performance. When a debate coach notes that your voice drops at the end of important points, they're giving you precise data that you can use to do better next time.

The most successful people in any field master this art of gathering and using feedback. This approach transforms random outcomes into reliable progress. Each piece of feedback adds another layer of understanding. What seemed like luck — *good or bad* — becomes a clear pattern you can adjust and improve. The more you understand these patterns, the more control you gain over your growth.

Sustaining Growth Through Challenges

Progress isn't a steady climb upward. Some days you surge ahead, mastering new skills and breaking through barriers. Other days you seem to slide backward, struggling with things that felt easy just yesterday. This inconsistency trips up many people who expect constant forward momentum.

Do not be confused or discouraged by this!

Think about learning a new song on guitar. One day, your fingers flow smoothly across the strings, hitting every note perfectly. The next day, you can barely remember where to place your hands. This isn't failure — it's your brain and body integrating new skills. Those apparent steps backward often precede significant breakthroughs.

The same pattern appears in every aspect of learning. Some days feel effortless and productive. Others feel like you're starting over from scratch. Understanding this pattern changes everything. Instead of getting discouraged by temporary setbacks, you begin to see them as natural rhythms in your growth. Those "*off days*" aren't failures — they're often signs that you're pushing your boundaries in precisely the right ways.

The key isn't to avoid these fluctuations but to work with them. Create systems that keep you moving forward even when motivation dips. Set aside specific times for practice. Prepare your environment to make showing up easier. Build in recovery periods — not as breaks from growth, but as essential parts of the process.

Most importantly, learn to measure progress over time rather than day to day. Look for trends across weeks and months rather than hours and days. Notice how setbacks often precede breakthroughs. Pay attention to how periods of apparent stagnation frequently lead to sudden improvements.

Remember: Growth isn't about perfection — *it's about persistence*. It's about getting back up after each setback, adjusting your approach when needed, and keeping your long-term direction even when the short-term path gets messy.

The Power of Shared Challenges

Growth might feel like a solitary journey, but the most significant breakthroughs often come through facing challenges together.

When we tackle complex tasks alone, it's easy to become overwhelmed or discouraged. With the right partners, those same challenges become opportunities for accelerated growth.

Our brains are wired for social learning. A challenging workout becomes more manageable with a training partner. An intricate piece of music feels more approachable when practiced with others. Complex problems become clearer when discussed with peers. This isn't coincidence — *it's human nature at work*.

The most effective growth partnerships balance challenge and support. They push us beyond our comfort zones while providing the encouragement needed to persist. Think of two students tackling advanced math problems together. They're sharing strategies, catching each other's mistakes, celebrating breakthroughs, and maintaining momentum when the problems get tough.

However, not all partnerships enhance growth. The key lies in finding people who

share both your commitment to improvement and your willingness to embrace challenges.

Look for partners who:

- Welcome difficult tasks as learning opportunities
- Support you through struggles while maintaining high standards
- Offer honest feedback with genuine encouragement
- Help analyze setbacks rather than avoid them
- Celebrate effort as much as success

The right partnership transforms how you approach challenges. Complex tasks become interesting puzzles to solve together. Setbacks become shared learning experiences. Progress accelerates as you benefit from each other's insights and experiences.

Understanding the Bigger Picture

Every significant challenge you face reshapes your capabilities in ways that extend far beyond the immediate task. Each new challenge you embrace adds capabilities that serve you in unexpected ways.

Consider these real-world examples:

A student who persistently tackles complex subjects isn't just *"book smart."* They're developing:

- The ability to break overwhelming challenges into manageable pieces
- Comfort with uncertainty and complex problems
- Resilience through repeated effort and adjustment
- Systematic approaches to learning and growth

These same capabilities later help them excel *in any challenging endeavor*, from starting a business to managing complex projects.

An athlete facing increasingly difficult training isn't just building physical skills. They're developing:

- The ability to push through discomfort productively
- Systematic approaches to improvement
- Recovery and adaptation strategies
- Mental toughness under pressure

Every challenge you face today prepares you for opportunities you can't yet imagine.

Think about that for a minute...

Those moments that push your limits, test your courage, and make your heart race — they're not just temporary obstacles...

They're the building blocks of your future self.

The courage you build facing one challenge becomes strength for more significant moments ahead. The resilience you develop through each setback transforms into an unshakeable core of confidence. The persistence you practice today becomes the power to pursue dreams you haven't even dreamed of yet!

Your future self will look back at these moments — not seeing the struggles, but recognizing them as the turning points where you began becoming who you were meant to be. What feels like a challenge today is actually the foundation of something extraordinary tomorrow.

TRY IT: Choose Discomfort

I'm going to make a wild guess that you're going to feel tempted to skip this activity. That *"I'd rather not"* feeling, is your limited mindset that's actively working to keep you comfortable, unchanged, and safe within your familiar *(but limiting)* patterns.

Can you feel yourself resisting?

If you can... *GOOD!*

This is an opportunity to take a step towards growth.

Choose a current challenge in your life — something that pushes you out of your comfort zone. It could be academic, athletic, social, or personal.

WRITE IT DOWN:

1. The challenge you want to tackle

2. One small step you'll take this week to face it

3. Someone who can support you along the way

Remember: The goal isn't perfection – *it's progress.*

By pushing past that initial resistance and writing it down, you've proven something critical to yourself:

You can choose growth over comfort!

Put this note somewhere you'll see it daily. Let it remind you that challenges aren't obstacles — **they're opportunities.**

Chapter 3
Learning From Criticism

"Criticism is something we can avoid easily by saying nothing, doing nothing, and being nothing." – Aristotle

You're standing at the front of the classroom, your presentation notes clutched in sweating hands. Your heart is racing. In a few moments, you'll have to present your project to your entire class.

The worst part, is that this isn't just a regular presentation. It's *a peer feedback session* where the other students get to weigh in and critique both your project and your presentation skills.

Your mind is spinning with panicked thoughts:

What if they don't understand my topic?

What if I stumble over my words?

What if they think my project is stupid?

Listening to criticism isn't easy, especially when you've poured hours of work into something that feels deeply personal. The thought of your classmates picking apart your presentation makes your stomach twist into knots.

But here's the truth: feedback isn't about tearing you down. It's about helping you grow stronger, more confident, and more skilled. Every comment - even the ones that sting a little - is an opportunity to see your work through fresh eyes.

Imagine if you could transform that wave of anxiety into excitement about improving. What if, instead of dreading criticism, you started seeing it as a secret weapon for becoming better?

When you learn to look past the initial discomfort and focus on the core message, feedback becomes less about highlighting flaws and more about encouraging progress. It's like having a mirror held up that shows you exactly where you can shine even brighter.

Types of Criticism: Constructive vs. Destructive

Picture this:

You've just finished a presentation in class. Your heart's still racing when your friend leans over and whispers, *"Hey, you had great ideas, but you were speaking so fast I missed some of them. Try slowing down next time?"*

That's **constructive criticism**.

Then there's the kid in the back who snickers, *"Wow, that was painful to watch."*

That's **destructive criticism**.

See the difference?

One points toward improvement. The other just points and laughs. One offers a specific observation and a path forward; the other is just empty, meaningless words.

Constructive criticism is like having a trusted advisor in your corner. When another classmate mentions, *"The research was solid, but maybe add some visuals next time to help us follow along,"* they're not just pointing out what could be better — they're showing you how to make it better. They're giving you specific tools to level up your presentation game.

Destructive criticism? It's more like having a heckler in the crowd. *"You suck"* or *"I was bored"* offers no guidance, no purpose, no value. It's just words meant to shake your confidence. These comments might sting, but they're empty.

When you know what real feedback looks like, you can filter out the noise and focus on what helps you grow. That comment about speaking too fast? It's a gift — specific, actionable information you can use next time. The snicker from the back of the room? That's just static on the radio — tune it out.

This skill becomes your secret weapon in all presentations moving forward. When your teacher suggests breaking up long sections with discussion questions, that's gold — try it next time. When they recommend practicing in front of a mirror to work on eye contact, that's another tool for your toolkit. When someone just says "*boring*," well, that tells you more about their small-minded limitations than anything that concerns you.

But here's where it gets interesting:

Learning to recognize good feedback doesn't just help you receive criticism better — it makes you better at giving it, too. Instead of telling a classmate, *"That was bad,"* you learn to say, *"The opening really grabbed my attention, but I lost track of the main points in the middle. Maybe try using transitions to connect your ideas?"* You become the kind of person who builds others up instead of tearing them down.

Think of it as developing your personal feedback filter. Every piece of criticism that comes your way goes through this filter. *"Try speaking slower"* — that's useful. *"Your voice sounds weird"* - that's meaningless noise that provides no value whatsoever.

This isn't just about surviving criticism — it's about using it as fuel for growth. Every piece of constructive feedback is a stepping stone toward becoming a more confident, skilled presenter. Every bit of destructive criticism becomes an opportunity to demonstrate resilience.

The real power comes when you start seeking out feedback instead of avoiding it. You begin to recognize that those moments of constructive criticism, though sometimes uncomfortable, are actually gold mines of opportunity.

Words have power. Constructive criticism harnesses that power for growth. Destructive criticism tries to use it for harm. Learning to tell the difference? That's real growth that you can use you're entire life.

The Power of Self-Reflection

Ever catch yourself replaying a moment in your mind? Maybe it's something someone said about your work, your ideas, your choices. The words echo, and suddenly, you're feeling all those emotions again.

This is where self-reflection begins.

Most people let these moments slip by, carrying the weight of criticism without examining what it means. Those who master self-reflection transform these echoes into insights.

Think about your last reaction to criticism. Really think about it.

Did you feel your defenses rise?

Did your mind start crafting comebacks before the person even finished speaking?

Or did you actually hear what they were saying?

Honest self-examination feels like cleaning out a closet – pulling everything into the light, examining each piece, and deciding what serves you.

Uncomfortable? *Yes.*

Transformative? *Absolutely.*

Try this: Next time you receive feedback, pause before reacting. Notice your immediate emotional response. Is your heart racing? Are your thoughts scattered? Are you already dismissing what you're hearing? These natural physical and emotional reactions reveal your deeper patterns.

Reflection Journaling

A reflection journal can be an invaluable tool to learn more about how you react to feedback. You can use an actual journal, a notebook, or even a note on your phone. Take note of both the feedback you receive and how you respond.

Look for patterns:

Do you reject criticism about specific topics?

Accept it more easily from some people than others?

React differently when you're stressed versus when you're calm?

Each journal entry adds another piece to your personal puzzle, revealing where you're growing and where you're stuck. Maybe you notice you instantly shut down when someone critiques your writing, but you're open to feedback about your athletic performance.

Why the difference?

What can one situation teach you about the other?

Self-reflection turns every piece of feedback into a mirror, revealing both others' perceptions and your own self-image. Catch those automatic, unhelpful thoughts:

- *"They just don't understand,"*
- *"I'll never be good enough,"*
- *"Why even try?"*

Challenge these thoughts. Question them. Control them.

Set aside dedicated time for this practice. Maybe Sunday evenings, or quiet moments before bed. Review recent feedback you've received, examining your responses:

- What was your first reaction?
- What did that reaction reveal?
- How might you respond differently now?

Over time, something remarkable happens. Your initial reactions to criticism begin to shift. That defensive wall lowers sooner. Your mind opens faster. You spot opportunities in critiques before feeling threatened.

Through self-reflection, each piece of feedback becomes a doorway to deeper understanding, transforming how you grow and learn.

Strategies to Handle and Absorb Criticism

Criticism can feel overwhelming, especially when emotions run high. Here are some ways to most effectively receive criticism:

- **Active listening is key**. When someone offers feedback, your first reaction might be to defend yourself. Instead, try focusing on understanding what's being said. One way to do this is by paraphrasing — or repeating back what you've heard in your own words. This approach shows that you're really trying to grasp the critique rather than just reacting negatively to it. For example, if your teacher says, "*Your report could use more detail,*" you might respond with, *"Are you saying I should add more specifics to make my point clearer?"* This simple technique clarifies the feedback and also opens up a conversation about how you can improve.
- **Emotional processing** is another essential part of managing criticism. You're not the only one who reacts emotionally to feedback. However, recognizing those emotional responses is crucial for self-awareness. You can always write down your feelings after receiving criticism. This will give you insight into why certain comments trigger specific emotions. I also find that taking a deep breath to calm my nerves works well. This reduces immediate emotional reaction. So, when you feel criticism is overwhelming you, close your eyes and take slow, deep breaths. This

small practice can shift your mood, allowing you to approach feedback more rationally.

- **Seek clarification** when feedback seems unclear or confusing. Questions are powerful tools for transforming vague critiques into actionable advice. If you receive criticism like, *"You need to learn to work better in a team,"* ask specific questions to get clarity. You might say, *"Can you give me an example of what I do that indicates I don't work well in teams?"* This not only helps you understand the issue but also provides clear steps on how to improve. Seeking clarity reduces misunderstandings and demonstrates a genuine interest in using criticism constructively.
- **Reframing critiques** is another strategy that can change how you perceive negative feedback. Looking at criticism from a different perspective can turn potentially demoralizing remarks into opportunities for growth. For instance, if a teacher says, *"Your presentation was too short,"* instead of thinking, *I failed,* try reframing it to, *"I have room to expand and include more information next time."* This shift in thinking helps transform negative feedback into a constructive tool, encouraging personal development rather than stifling your progress.

Putting It All Together

Like learning any new skill, it takes practice to get comfortable with criticism. The more you use these tools, the more natural they become.

Think about a musician learning a complex piece of music. They don't tackle the entire song at once — they break it down into manageable sections. Similarly, you don't have to become a feedback master overnight. Start with one piece of criticism. Apply your filter. Practice your active listening. Try your reframing techniques.

Each time you face feedback, you have a choice:

- *A) Fall back into old patterns*
- *B) Try a new approach*

Every small success builds confidence. Every challenge becomes an opportunity to refine your skills.

Remember that presentation example from earlier? The next time you're in a similar situation, you'll be ready. You'll have your feedback filter in place. You'll know how to separate valuable insights from empty criticism. Most importantly, you'll understand that each piece of constructive feedback is another step toward your goals.

Ready to put these ideas into practice?

Let's start with a simple exercise...

TRY IT: The Feedback Filter

Take the next 10 minutes to test your new feedback filter. Think of the last time someone gave you feedback – good or bad, big or small. Maybe it was about a presentation, an assignment, or even your gaming skills. Got it in mind? Good.

1. First, write down exactly what they said. Don't soften it or make it nicer — put down their exact words.
2. Now comes the interesting part. Let's sort this feedback using your new filter. What part of their comment was actually valuable — something specific you could act on? Write that down.
3. What part was just noise, vague criticism, or unhelpful comments?
4. Finally, take the valuable part and turn it into one specific action you could take to improve. Make it something concrete you could start doing this week.

That's it! You've just practiced one of life's most valuable skills — filtering feedback to find the gold and let the gravel fall away.

Chapter 4
Building Resilience

*Hardships often prepare ordinary people for
an extraordinary destiny.* –C.S. Lewis

Imagine this: Everything you prepared for, everything you worked toward, just fell apart in spectacular fashion. Your face burns with embarrassment. Your confidence is shattered. And right now, you have to make a choice:

Let this moment break you, or find a way to come back stronger.

This is where resilience begins.

Not the fluffy, motivational-poster kind of resilience that tells you to "*keep smiling*" or "*everything happens for a reason.*" We're talking about real resilience — the kind that turns crushing defeats into comeback fuel. The kind that doesn't just help you survive tough moments, but teaches you how to rise from them stronger than before.

Every person you admire has stood precisely where you're standing. They've felt that same burning embarrassment, that same shattered confidence, that same urge to disappear. What sets them apart isn't that they never failed — *it's what they chose to do next.*

Real Stories Of Resilience

Resilience doesn't just help you survive trying moments — it transforms them into stepping stones for growth. History is packed with people who faced enormous, seemingly unbeatable odds and came out stronger. Their stories are proof that resilience isn't just a nice idea. It's profoundly transformative.

Consider the story of Nelson Mandela. Picture a young man in South Africa, standing up to apartheid; a brutal system that treated Black citizens as less than human. Mandela believed in equality so fiercely that he spent 27 years in prison for it. Imagine losing nearly three decades of your life, locked away, with no guarantee that freedom would ever come. Even against terrible odds, Mandela didn't let prison break him. Instead, he used it as a classroom. He read, strategized, and prepared for the moment he could lead others. When he finally walked free, Mandela became South Africa's first Black president, using his position to unite a divided nation and steer it toward equality. His resilience didn't just free him — it helped free a country.

Or take Anne Frank. She wasn't a world leader; she was a teenager, just like you. During World War II, Anne and her family hid in a cramped attic for over two years, trying to avoid Nazi persecution. Imagine never being able to go outside, living in constant fear, with every sound potentially giving you away. But Anne didn't let fear consume her. Instead, she wrote. In her diary, she poured out her hopes, her frustrations, and her belief that people were still good at heart. Her resilience turned her private thoughts into one of the most powerful testaments to human courage the world has ever known through *"The Diary Of Anne Frank."*

And then there's Malala Yousafzai. Growing up in Pakistan, she loved school, but extremists in her town didn't think girls should be educated. Malala refused to stay silent. She spoke out, knowing it made her a target. When she was just 15, an attacker tried to silence her permanently. But Malala's story didn't end there. She survived, and she didn't just recover — she came back louder, stronger, and more determined than ever. By the age of 17, she had become the youngest person to win the Nobel Peace Prize, inspiring millions to fight for education and equality.

Here's the thing about these stories: they're not just about surviving — they're about choosing growth. Mandela didn't just endure prison; he transformed it into a foundation for leadership. Anne didn't let her confinement crush her spirit; she turned it into a legacy of hope. Malala didn't let violence stop her; she turned it into fuel for change.

This is what resilience looks like. It's not an absence of fear or struggle, but a refusal to let those things define you. And it's not reserved for world leaders, activists, or historical icons. It's in the everyday moments, too.

Maybe for you, it's raising your hand in class when you're not 100% sure of the answer. Or trying out for the team after last year's rejection. Or reaching out to someone new, knowing they might say no. Or standing up for what you know is right, even in the face of difficult circumstances. These moments matter because this is how resilience is built. One small act of courage at a time.

Building Your Resilience Muscles

Think of resilience like a muscle. You wouldn't walk into a gym and try to lift the heaviest weights on day one. Instead, you build strength gradually, consistently, one rep at a time.

The same goes for resilience. It's built through daily habits, small choices, and regular practice. Each time you face a challenge, push through discomfort or bounce back from a setback, you're building that strength.

The Power of Routine

Chaos hits differently when you've got a solid foundation. That's what routine gives you. Not the boring, repetitive kind, but a rhythm that keeps you steady when everything else feels shaky.

When your world turns upside down, having certain anchors — maybe your morning playlist, your evening run, or even just your specific way of organizing your backpack — these become your secret weapons against uncertainty. It's like having a personal force field that helps you stay focused when everything around you goes crazy.

Start small. Maybe it's setting your alarm 15 minutes earlier to have some quiet time. Or creating a study ritual that feels more like self-care than a chore. Build your morning routine one piece at a time. Add an evening wind-down that helps you reflect and recharge. To establish a supportive routine, the key isn't perfection. It's consistency.

These routines become your foundation. When tough times hit, they're the steady ground you stand on. They remind you that even when some things are out of control, you still have power over how you approach each day.

The Challenge Game

Real growth happens just outside your comfort zone. That space where your heart beats a little faster, your palms get a bit sweaty, but something inside you whispers, "*let's give it a try.*"

We're not talking about massive, terrifying leaps. Think small steps that make your heart beat just a little faster. Raising your hand in class when you're not 100%

sure. Starting a conversation with someone new. Trying that sport you've always watched from the sidelines. Sharing your art even though it's not *"perfect."*

Each small challenge you take on is like a rep for your resilience muscles. Every time you push past that initial *"nope, can't do it"* feeling, you're getting stronger. The key is to start small and build up. Maybe today it's answering one question in class. Next week, it's volunteering for a presentation. The month after? Leading a group project.

The Reflection Revolution

Your mind is constantly telling you stories about yourself. But are you listening? Really listening?

We've talked about journaling a bit already — not the *"dear diary"* kind, but the kind that helps you understand your own story better. Write about your challenges, your victories, even your face-plants.

What worked?

What didn't?

What would you try differently next time?

These aren't just words on a page. They're the blueprint of your growth that helps you gradually build up your personal resilience over time.

Flipping the Failure Script

That test you bombed? That tryout that went sideways? That social situation that still makes you cringe? They're not endpoints — they're data points. Each one tells you something useful about what to try next.

Stop seeing failure as a wall. Start seeing it as feedback. Every *"mistake"* is actually information about what to adjust, what to rethink, and what to try differently next time. It's like having a GPS for growth. When you take a wrong turn, it doesn't yell at you; it just recalculates and shows you a new route.

This isn't about positive thinking or pretending setbacks don't hurt. It's about training yourself to ask better questions:

"What can I learn from this?" instead of *"Why did this happen to me?"*

"How can I adjust?" instead of *"What's wrong with me?"*

Think about any skill you've mastered. Maybe it's a video game, a sport, or an instrument. You didn't get good by getting everything right the first time, did you?

You got good by trying, failing, adjusting, and trying again. Each failure taught you something new about how to succeed.

Remember, every resilient person you admire started precisely where you are — building their resilience one small habit at a time. They felt the same fears, faced the same doubts, and made the same mistakes. What set them apart wasn't natural talent or luck. It was their willingness to keep going, keep learning, and keep growing.

Building Your Support System

Think of the last time everything felt too heavy to handle alone. That moment when your confidence cracked, when the challenge seemed too big, when giving up felt like the only option.

Now, imagine having a team in your corner. Not just cheerleaders, but people who genuinely get it. People who know how to help you turn setbacks into comebacks.

This is where your support network comes in.

Your Resilience Team

A strong support system isn't just about having people around – it's about having *the right people* around. The ones who:

- See your struggle, but believe in your strength
- Listen without judgment but push you toward growth
- Share their own battle stories and how they made it through
- Remind you of your progress when you can only see how far you have to go

These aren't just friends — they're your resilience builders. When your confidence wavers, they hold that belief for you until you can reclaim it.

Finding Your People

Building this network takes intention. It's about recognizing who makes you stronger and who drains your resilience reserves.

Look for people who've faced similar challenges and come out stronger. Their experience isn't just inspiring, it's also a roadmap you can learn from.

Mentors who push you beyond your comfort zone while showing you how to handle the discomfort. Maybe it's that coach who knows exactly when to push and when to support. Or that teacher who sees potential in you that you haven't discovered yet. Friends who make space for both your struggles and your triumphs. The ones who let you vent, but don't let you stay stuck. The ones who celebrate your wins without competing. The ones who remind you of your strength when you forget.

Being a Resilience Builder

Here's something powerful:

While you're building your support network, you're also learning to be that support for others. When you share your struggles and victories, you're showing others what resilience looks like in action.

This isn't about having all the answers. It's about being present, being honest, and being willing to grow together. When you help someone else push through a challenging moment, you're actually strengthening your own resilience muscles, too.

Remember, no one builds resilience alone. Even the strongest people you know have a support system. They've learned that true strength isn't about handling everything solo. It's about knowing when to lean on others and how to help them lean on you.

Your resilience journey is unique to you, but you don't have to walk it alone. Start building your team today. Look around.

- Who makes you feel stronger?
- Who helps you bounce back?
- Who shows you what's possible?

Those are your people. That's your team. And together, you're all becoming more resilient, one challenge at a time.

The Long-Term Benefits of Support Network

Studies show that people with strong social connections have better mental health, lower stress levels, and even longer lifespans. A good support network reminds you that you're not alone, no matter how tough life gets.

On the flip side, isolation can make challenges feel insurmountable. Without people to rely on, stress and uncertainty can become overwhelming, leading to feelings of helplessness.

Resilience doesn't mean handling everything on your own — it means knowing when to ask for help and who to ask. By investing in your support network, you're not just preparing for the hard times; you're also building a foundation for success, joy, and growth.

TRY IT: Strengthen Your Resilience

Resilience isn't just about tackling challenges head-on — it's also about knowing when to lean on others and offering support in return. Take these three steps to build and strengthen your support network while practicing resilience:

Step 1: Identify Your Support Circle

Grab a notebook or open a notes app and create a simple list of the people in your life who uplift and inspire you.

Think of:

- Friends who make you feel heard and valued
- Teachers, mentors, or coaches who push you to grow
- Family members who support you unconditionally

Once your list is ready, reflect on how each person has helped you in the past. Do they give great advice? Are they good at listening? Acknowledging their strengths will remind you of the connections you already have and the resilience they've helped you build.

Step 2: Strengthen One Connection

Choose one person from your list and make an effort to deepen your bond. This could mean:

- Inviting a friend to hang out face-to-face (grab a coffee, go for a walk, or just chill together).
- Writing a heartfelt thank-you note to someone who's been there for you during tough times.
- Opening up about a current challenge and asking for advice or support.

Building stronger relationships doesn't have to be complicated—it's about showing others you value them and are willing to invest in your connection.

Step 3: Be a Resilience Builder for Someone Else

Now, flip the script. Think of someone who might need *your* support this week. Maybe it's a friend struggling with school, a sibling feeling overwhelmed, or even a classmate who seems a little down.

Do one small thing to show them you care:

- Offer to help with a problem they're facing.
- Check-in with a quick text or phone call. (Something simple, like *"Hey, how are you holding up?"*)
- Celebrate something they've accomplished recently.

Being there for others strengthens your resilience by reinforcing empathy, problem-solving, and connection.

Chapter 5
Self-Reflection and Goal Setting

"If you don't know yourself, you don't know anything."
– Socrates

Imagine this:

You're standing at a crossroads of potential. On one side, a path of familiar comfort. On the other, a trail of unknown challenges and untapped possibilities. Your heart races with a mix of excitement and uncertainty.

Maybe it's a dream you've been hesitating to pursue. A skill you've always wanted to master. A goal that feels just beyond your reach. The potential is there, humming with energy, but something keeps holding you back. A whisper of doubt. A fear of failure. The uncomfortable feeling of stepping outside your comfort zone.

We've all been there. Staring at that invisible barrier between where we are and where we want to be. Close enough to see the possibility, but somehow unable to take that first step.

You might tell yourself;

"This would be so much easier, IF ONLY..."

It's a natural human trait to wish for more ideal circumstances. We spend our lives wanting the world to change. Wanting easier challenges, better situations, different rules, or an advantage. We tend to blame our struggles on everything around us. Bad luck. Unfair teachers. Impossible situations.

The simple fact of the matter is that there's only one thing that you can control...

Yourself.

This is where self-reflection begins. Not the vague *"think about your feelings"* kind of reflection. We're talking about the powerful practice of truly understanding yourself, your reactions, your patterns, and your unique way of seeing the world. It's about learning to read your own story just as carefully as you'd read someone else's.

Every incredible journey starts with self-understanding. Whether you're trying to write a story, choose a career path, or figure out why certain situations always seem to trip you up. The ability to look inward with honesty and curiosity is one of the most powerful skills you can master. While others are fruitlessly demanding the world adapt to them, you'll be building the self-awareness that lets you adapt, grow, and ultimately reshape the world around you.

The first step is <u>*self-reflection*</u>. It's about pausing to examine your thoughts, actions, and motivations — uncovering the patterns that guide your decisions.

The second step is <u>*goal-setting*</u>. Attaining the ability to craft a set of intentional, meaningful, attainable goals that transform your insights into action — and your action into results.

By combining self-reflection with goal-setting, you create a powerful loop of growth. Reflection helps you understand where you are, and goal-setting shows you where to go. Together, they provide the tools to navigate life's crossroads, making each decision purposeful and aligned with the future you want to build.

The Power of Self-Reflection

Self-reflection is like holding up a mirror. Not to judge yourself, but to truly see yourself. It's an active practice of understanding why you think, feel, and act the way you do. Without it, you're like a traveler without a map, wandering aimlessly through life's choices and challenges. With it, you become a navigator of your journey, equipped to chart a path that's both purposeful and fulfilling.

Think about it: every decision you make and every interaction you have stems from how you see yourself and the world around you. If you don't take the time to reflect, those choices can feel random or disconnected. But when you pause to look inward, you gain clarity. You start to see patterns — how you react to stress, what motivates you, and where you tend to get stuck. These insights become the foundation for growth.

<u>*Why*</u> Self-Reflection Matters

Your "*why*" is the core purpose that drives everything you do. It's deeper than just goals or achievements — it's the fundamental reason behind your actions, the values that light you up inside, and the impact you want to make in the world.

Think of your "*why*" as your internal compass. It's the answer to the most critical question you can ask yourself:

"Why do I do what I do?"

For some people, their "*why*" might be about making a difference in their community. For others, it could be about personal growth, creativity, or supporting their family.

Let's break it down with an example. Say you're passionate about environmental protection. Your surface-level goal might be to recycle or join an environmental club. But your deeper "*why*" could be about preserving the planet for future generations, or feeling a connection to the natural world, or believing that every individual can create meaningful change.

When you're clear about your "*why,*" decisions become easier. Challenges become more manageable. Setbacks don't derail you because you understand the larger purpose driving your actions. It's like having an internal navigation system that keeps you focused and motivated, even when the path gets tough.

Without a clear "*why,*" you might find yourself:

- Feeling constantly scattered
- Pursuing goals that don't truly excite you
- Losing motivation quickly
- Struggling to make meaningful choices

But when you connect with your "*why,*" everything changes. Your actions become more intentional. Your energy becomes more focused. Your life starts to feel more meaningful and aligned.

Self-reflection is the key to uncovering this powerful purpose. It's about digging beneath the surface, asking yourself the tough questions, and discovering what truly matters to you.

The Three Pillars of Reflection

To start reflecting effectively, focus on three key areas:

1) Your Patterns

Take a look at the habits and behaviors that define your daily life.

Do you procrastinate when faced with enormous tasks?

Do you recognize any bad habits that you'd be better off without?

Do you thrive under pressure or crumble under stress?

Identifying these patterns helps you understand what's working and what's holding you back.

2) Your Triggers

Everyone has emotional triggers — situations or comments that spark strong reactions. Maybe you feel defensive when someone critiques your work, or you get overwhelmed when plans change suddenly. Reflection helps you pinpoint these triggers and uncover the beliefs behind them, giving you the power to respond thoughtfully instead of reacting impulsively.

3) Your Values

What truly matters to you? What motivates you to keep going, even when things get tough? Reflecting on your values helps you align your decisions with what's most important, creating a sense of purpose that guides your actions.

How to Start Reflecting

Self-reflection doesn't require hours of meditation or deep philosophical musings. It starts with simple questions, asked with curiosity rather than judgment:

- What's been working well lately, and why?
- What challenges did I face, and how did I handle them?
- What did I learn about myself from this experience?

Even five minutes a day spent journaling or thinking about these questions can lead to powerful insights. Over time, you'll start to notice themes — things that consistently energize or drain you, strategies that help you succeed, and habits that hold you back.

Turning Reflection into Action

Reflection isn't just about understanding yourself. You have to use that understanding to make better choices. Once you've identified a pattern or learned something new about yourself, ask:

- How can I use this insight to improve?
- What's one small change I can make today?

For example, if you realize that you're most productive in the morning, you might start scheduling your most demanding tasks for that time. If you notice that negative self-talk often creeps in before significant challenges, you could practice reframing those thoughts with affirmations like, *"I've prepared for this, and I can handle it."*

Reflection gives you the tools to take ownership of your growth. Instead of feeling stuck or overwhelmed, you start to see each moment as an opportunity to learn and adapt.

Setting Life-Changing Goals

Understanding challenges is essential. But creating meaningful change requires something more:

Structured , intentional, methodical **action**.

This is where S.M.A.R.T. goal-setting becomes invaluable. It's an acronym that stands for **S**pecific, **M**easurable, **A**chievable, **R**elevant, **T**ime-Bound.

Think of it not as a rigid formula, but as a framework for turning aspirations into tangible achievements.

Let's say you want to learn how to drive a car. Here is an example of how you can create this goal using the S.M.A.R.T. framework:

Specific: *"I want to learn how to drive*" sounds straightforward until you actually sit behind the wheel. What exactly do you need to learn? A *specific* goal breaks this down into clear skills:

"I want to master the essential driving skills for my license test – smooth acceleration and braking, precise steering, parallel parking, highway merging, and navigating intersections safely."

Now, THAT's a specific goal. You're not just *"learning to drive"* – you're developing specific abilities that add up to you becoming a competent driver. This clarity helps you focus your practice time effectively instead of wondering what to work on next.

Measurable: Just counting hours behind the wheel doesn't tell you if you're improving. You need concrete ways to track progress. For parallel parking, count how many attempts you need to park correctly. For highway driving, track how smoothly you maintain your speed and position in your lane. For general skills, note how often your parent or instructor needs to give corrections during each practice session.

These *measurements* transform vague progress into clear data. Instead of wondering if you're getting better, you'll know exactly where you've improved and what still needs work.

Achievable: While you might dream of driving like an expert immediately, rushing into advanced skills is a recipe for frustration. Start with mastering the basics in empty parking lots. Smooth starts and stops, turning with precision, backing straight. Once these feel natural, move to quiet residential streets. Build up to busier roads only when you're consistently handling quieter ones well.

This gradual progression keeps you challenged without becoming overwhelmed, which helps the task remain *achievable*. Each small success builds confidence for the next step, creating momentum rather than anxiety.

Relevant: Connect your driving goals to what matters in your life. Maybe you want to help with family errands, drive yourself to school or work, or gain more independence. Think about specific, *relevant* trips you'd like to make or responsibilities you'd like to take on.

These personal connections provide motivation during challenging moments. When you're struggling to master a particular skill, remembering why it matters to you personally helps maintain your determination.

Time-bound: Without deadlines, practice can drift aimlessly. Create a realistic timeline that drives steady progress: First two weeks for parking lot basics. Next three weeks for residential streets. Following four weeks for busier roads and highway practice. Final three weeks for perfecting all skills before your test.

These deadlines create urgency while remaining realistic. They help you pace your learning and ensure you're making consistent progress toward your goal.

Putting It All Together

Initial goal: *"Learn how to drive."*

S.M.A.R.T. Version:

'Complete 40 hours of supervised driving practice over the next three months. Master basic car control in empty lots during weeks 1-2, residential driving in weeks 3-5, busy streets in weeks 6-9, and highway driving in weeks 10-12.

Practice parallel parking for 15 minutes each session until I can park successfully 8 out of 10 times. Complete practice driving test with instructor by week 11, focusing week 12 on any weak areas. Pass official driving test by end of month three."

This structured approach transforms an intimidating goal into clear, actionable steps. Each element of SMART works together, creating a realistic path from complete beginner to licensed driver.

In the end, it's about progress. By breaking down your biggest goals into clear, measurable steps, you create a map for success. Each small achievement builds confidence. Each setback provides valuable feedback. Step by step, what once seemed impossible becomes inevitable.

Reflection Journaling

Think of every experience as a story waiting to be understood. That impressive presentation you nailed. That test that totally went sideways. That moment when everything clicked in practice. Each one holds clues about how you learn, grow, and perform at your best.

Don't get hung up on the format. Whether it's a leather-bound notebook, a notes app on your phone, or a document in the cloud – what matters is that you can capture insights when they're fresh and review them when you need guidance.

The Art of Capturing Moments

Imagine you just finished a major presentation. Instead of just feeling relieved it's over, take a moment to record what happened:

"History presentation today. Started shaky – hands trembling during first slide. But found my rhythm after the introduction. Audience seemed really engaged during the personal story section. Lost my place once but recovered by asking the class a question while I gathered my thoughts."

That's a nice start, but break it down even further:

- What worked? *The personal story grabbed attention*
- What challenged you? *The opening moments, losing your place*
- How did you adapt? *Turning a stumble into audience engagement*
- What would you do differently? *Maybe start with the story next time*

The big difference here is that you're not just remembering what happened – *you're actively learning from it.* Maybe you discover that starting with your strongest material helps you find confidence faster. Or that connecting with your audience makes you less focused on your nervousness.

Expanding Your Awareness

Over time, expand on your entries and go even deeper by creating different sections in your journal:

Performance Patterns: Notice how different approaches affect your results. Maybe you discover you understand math concepts better when you draw them out visually. Or that you retain information longer when you explain it to someone else. These aren't just random observations – they're clues about how your mind works best.

Energy Patterns: Track when you feel most alert, creative, or focused. You might find you solve problems better in the morning, or that your creativity peaks late at night. This isn't just interesting – it's valuable data about when to tackle different types of challenges.

Environmental Factors: Note which conditions help or hinder your performance. Background music might help you focus on some tasks but distract you during others. Certain study spots might energize you, while others make you sleepy.

Using Your Insights

Here's where most people stop. They collect observations but never use them. Your journal should be more than just a record to look back on – it should be a tool for active improvement.

When you notice a pattern, design an experiment:

- If background music helps you focus, create specific playlists for different types of work
- If you understand concepts better by teaching them, start a study group
- If you perform better after one particular warm-up routine, make it a non-negotiable part of your preparation

This is taking what you learned about yourself and then setting yourself up for even greater levels of success by controlling as many elements as possible. It's putting the knowledge that you're learning about yourself to use as best as possible to maximize your results.

Making It a Habit

Set specific times for journaling:

- Quick notes right after important events
- Weekly review to spot patterns
- Monthly reflection to plan adjustments

Create prompts that help you dig deeper:

- What surprised me this week?
- What patterns am I noticing?
- What experiments should I try next?
- What's working that I should do more of?

The Bigger Picture

Over time, this practice transforms growth from random improvement into strategic development. Each experience becomes more than just a moment – it becomes a lesson, a stepping stone, a piece of the puzzle that is you.

Your journal will become your personal manual for success, written one insight at a time. It really is a lot like creating an instruction manual for yourself — the trick is that you have to figure out how you work in order to write it.

Your journal reveals not just what you're capable of, but also how to access your best performance consistently. It shows you not just where you want to go, but also the specific steps that will take you to get there.

This isn't just about getting better – it's about understanding the unique way you get better. It's about turning your growth from guesswork into science, from hope into strategy, from random progress into deliberate development.

TRY IT: Your First Self-Discovery Page

Think about something that happened this week that triggered a strong reaction in you – *good or bad*. Maybe you crushed a presentation. Perhaps you backed away from a challenge. Maybe something small bothered you more than it should have.

Write down:

1. What exactly happened: _____
2. How you reacted (thoughts, feelings, actions): _____
3. One pattern this might reveal about you: _____

That's it! You've just written your first growth journal entry. Place it somewhere you'll see it every day.

Remember: Understanding yourself isn't something that spontaneously occurs — it happens one intentional moment of awareness at a time.

Chapter 6
Building Unshakeable Self-Belief

"Whether you think you can, or you think you can't – you're right."
– Henry Ford

Imagine this:

You're scrolling through social media late at night. Each swipe reveals another perfectly curated moment from someone else's life. A friend crushing their dance recital. Your classmate celebrating another academic award. That girl from math class living what looks like a dream life.

And there you are, in your quiet room, feeling somehow... less.

Why can't I be more like them?

This thought – this exact moment of comparison and self-doubt – is where most people get stuck. They let these feelings of *"not enough"* define them, limit them, and hold them back.

Most people don't understand that self-belief isn't some magical confidence that certain people are born with. Believing in yourself is not about never feeling scared or uncertain — and it's definitely not about being perfect.

Self-belief is about understanding a simple but powerful truth:

You don't have to be perfect to be worthy. You don't have to have it all figured out to take the next step. You don't have to feel ready to begin.

Look at anyone who's achieved something remarkable – in sports, academics, business, art, or anything. What separates them from those who gave up?

It's the simple choice to keep going when others would quit.

There's a word for someone who refuses to give up — *unstoppable.*

Who can defeat someone who, despite doubts and setbacks, always finds a way to take one more step forward?

This unstoppable quality doesn't come from being fearless – it comes from having unshakeable belief in yourself and your ability to find a way through.

The biggest obstacle you'll ever face isn't the challenge in front of you. *It's the doubt inside you.*

Master that, and you become *unstoppable.*

The Power of Affirmations

Your inner voice is the most consistent narrator in your life. It comments on your choices, judges your performance, and all too often, questions your worth. Left unchecked, it tends to echo the same doubts and fears on repeat:

I'll never get this right.

I'm not good enough.

That kind of recurring negative thinking is what tends to bury people in a hole that they dug for themselves without even knowing it, BUT... there's good news...

That little voice can be reprogrammed to be positive!

It can be reshaped. It can become your greatest coach and your most loyal cheerleader. To reshape and reprogram that little voice in your head, we use a simple, but effective tool called *affirmations.*

What Exactly Are Affirmations?

Affirmations are positive statements you choose to repeat to yourself. They're designed to challenge negative beliefs and build mental resilience. They help you focus on your strengths, your potential, and the steps you can take to improve.

Think of affirmations as a steering wheel for your thoughts. Without them, your mind can easily veer into negative territory, reinforcing limiting beliefs like *"I can't do this."* But with affirmations, you consciously steer your thinking toward growth and possibility.

Affirmations work because your brain is constantly creating and reinforcing neural pathways. When you repeatedly think, *"I'm not capable,"* your brain strengthens that pathway, making it easier to think that same thought again and again. Affirmations interrupt this process. They carve out new pathways — ones rooted in self-belief, confidence, and resilience. Over time, these new pathways become the default.

What Makes a Great Affirmation?

Not all affirmations are effective. The most powerful ones meet you where you are but point toward where you want to go. They should feel believable, even if they stretch your comfort zone a little. If an affirmation feels like a lie, your brain will reject it, and it won't stick.

Here's the difference:

- Ineffective: *"I'm amazing at everything!"*
- Effective: *"I'm improving a little more every day."*

Good affirmations acknowledge the journey while reinforcing your ability to grow. Some good examples:

- *"Every challenge I face helps me grow stronger."*
- *"I am capable of figuring things out."*
- *"I'm learning and improving through every experience."*
- *"I face tough situations with courage and determination."*

These statements don't demand perfection. Instead, they encourage progress and resilience.

Overcoming Negative Self-Talk

We all have moments when our inner voice turns critical.

- *"I'm so bad at this."*
- *"I always mess up."*
- *"Why do I even try?"*

These thoughts can feel automatic and overwhelming, but they're not as immovable as they seem.

44

When a negative thought surfaces, don't try to shove it away. That often makes it stronger. Instead, approach it with curiosity.

Ask yourself:

- *Where did this thought come from?*
- *Is it really true?*
- *What evidence do I have for or against it?*

Once you've examined the thought, reframe it in a way that focuses on growth. For example:

- Negative: *"I always fail at presentations."*
- Reframed: *"I'm learning to become a stronger presenter every time I try."*

It's all about changing the way you look at struggles and negativity and then reframing them so that they can be used as fuel for growth and improvement. The thing is, these thoughts are going to be used for something either way... *either tearing you down or building you up...* so you might as well **choose** to have them working for you rather than against you.

Integrating Affirmations into Your Life

Affirmations only work if they're practiced consistently. Think of them as mental workouts. Just like physical exercise builds muscle, repeating affirmations builds stronger, more resilient thought patterns.

1) Start Your Day with Intention: Begin each morning by saying two or three affirmations that resonate with you. Take a moment to breathe deeply and focus on the meaning behind the words.

For example:

- *"I am capable of handling today's challenges."*
- *"I am growing stronger and wiser every day."*

2) Use Affirmations as Reset Buttons: When you're about to face a challenge — like a test, a presentation, or a difficult conversation — hit the reset button. Take a deep breath and repeat your affirmations. This will help you center and find your focus so that you can proceed onwards with the confidence of knowing that no matter the outcome of the challenge at hand, it's going to benefit you.

3) Reflect at the End of the Day: Before bed, revisit your affirmations and think about how they shaped your actions.

Ask yourself:

- *How did I embody these beliefs today?*
- *What can I do tomorrow to live them more fully?*

4) Anchor Them in Your Environment: Write your affirmations where you'll see them often: on sticky notes, in your planner, or as a phone background. Let them become part of your everyday surroundings.

Pairing Affirmations with Action

Affirmations are not magic. They don't work <u>unless you do</u>. Their real power comes when you pair them with effort.

You can say, *"I'm going to have 6-pack abs"* a million times, but unless you pair it with putting in the work, nothing is going to happen.

If you tell yourself, *"I'm prepared for this exam,"* back it up by studying diligently.

If you affirm, *"I can handle difficult conversations,"* take the time to plan what you'll say and practice staying calm.

When you combine affirmations with action, you create a powerful, positive feedback loop. The more you act on your affirmations, the more believable they become. And the more you believe them, the more motivated you are to take action. The more action you take, the closer you get to your goals. You see how it works.

Why Affirmations Are Worth It

At first, affirmations might feel awkward or forced, especially if your inner critic has been running the show for a long time. But stick with it. Over time, they'll feel less like something you're trying and more like something you are.

Imagine replacing *"I'm not good enough"* with *"I'm figuring this out."* Surely you see how that shift could change the way you approach challenges, setbacks, and even everyday moments?

Affirmations don't erase struggles — they help you navigate them with strength and clarity. They transform your inner voice from a source of doubt into a source of encouragement. Every time you choose an affirmation that reinforces your potential, you're taking a small but powerful step toward becoming the person you're meant to be.

Visualization: Training Your Mind

Tomorrow's presentation has been looming over you for weeks. But instead of letting anxiety take over, you're about to learn a powerful tool that champions use to perform at their best.

Close your eyes.

Take a slow breath.

Now play the scene vividly in your mind:

You're walking confidently to the front of the room, each step purposeful and strong. Your classmates' eyes are on you, and instead of that familiar knot of fear, you feel something electric coursing through you – a mixture of excitement, purpose, and readiness. Your shoulders are back, head high, a slight smile playing at your lips because you know something they don't: **You've got this.**

You've prepared for this moment. Every word, every gesture, every slide is locked into your mind. As you turn to face the class, you feel centered, grounded, and entirely in control. Your opening line flows out precisely as you practiced. Your voice is strong and clear, carrying naturally to the back of the room. You see heads nodding, faces lighting up with interest. Some students even lean forward in their seats, drawn in by your energy and confidence.

Time seems to slow down as you hit your stride. Each point lands perfectly. Your gestures feel natural, emphasizing key ideas exactly when they should. When you pause for effect, the silence holds perfect tension. You're not just giving a presentation – you're commanding the room, sharing something valuable — making a powerful, positive impact.

This isn't just daydreaming. This is mental rehearsal. Olympic athletes use this exact technique before competing, musicians before performances, and surgeons before complex procedures. You're not just imagining success; you're actively programming your brain for it.

When you visualize an action with enough detail and emotion, your brain creates neural pathways similar to those formed during actual practice. Think about that for a minute: You're essentially giving yourself extra rehearsal time, building muscle memory without moving a muscle. Elite performers in every field use this exact technique *because it works.*

47

But here's the key: Visualization isn't about pretending everything will be perfect. It's about preparing yourself to handle whatever comes your way. In your mental rehearsal, include how you'll handle challenges:

- A little stumble as you walk to the front
- A question you weren't expecting
- A moment where you lose your place
- A distraction in the room

See yourself handling each situation with calm confidence. Because when these moments come in real life *(and they will)*, your brain will recognize them and know what to do.

Making It Real: A Step Beyond Imagining

Champions don't just visualize occasionally. They make it a systematic practice. Think of it like building mental muscle. Just as athletes follow a training schedule, you need a visualization routine that works for you:

Find your time: Maybe it's right before bed, when your mind is quiet. Or during your morning shower, when ideas flow freely. Or on the bus to school, with your headphones creating a bubble of focus. Pick a consistent time when you can immerse yourself undisturbed.

Make it vivid: Engage all your senses. What do you see? The faces in the crowd, the setup of the room, the slides on the screen. What do you hear? The sound of your voice, the rustle of movement, the silence of attention. What do you feel? The temperature of the room, your feet planted firmly, your breathing steady and controlled. The more detail you include, the more powerful the practice becomes.

Feel it: Don't just see yourself succeeding — *feel* the emotions. The confidence flows through you when you nail your opening. The satisfaction of fielding a tricky question smoothly. The pride of finishing strong and knowing you gave it your all.

Capturing the Vision

This is where journaling, again, is incredibly powerful. After each visualization session, write down what you saw, felt, and learned. This is an essential step because it's reinforcing the neural pathways you're building.

Create specific journal entries:

- What scenarios did you visualize?
- Which parts felt most real?

- What strategies did you imagine using?
- How did you handle challenges in your mental rehearsal?
- What emotions came up during the practice?

Over time, these journal entries become a personal playbook for success. You'll start noticing patterns: which visualization techniques work best for you, which challenges you've prepared for, and which areas need more mental practice.

The Compound Effect

Think of each visualization session, each journal entry, and each small win as a deposit in your confidence bank. Over time, these deposits compound. Your mental rehearsals become more detailed and effective. Your ability to handle challenges improves. Your belief in yourself grows stronger.

This is how real, lasting confidence is built. Not through empty affirmations or wishful thinking, but through systematic mental preparation and recognition of your progress.

When the big moment comes — whether it's a presentation, performance, or competition — you're not just walking in with hope. You're walking in with *evidence-based confidence*. You've already succeeded dozens of times in your mind. You've documented your capabilities. You've proven to yourself that you can handle challenges.

This is how champions are made. Not in the moment of performance, but in the countless moments of preparation that came before. Mental preparation is just as important as physical practice. Sometimes, it's even more important.

Every time you practice visualization, you're not just preparing for one moment — you're building a skill that will serve you in every challenge you face. You're developing the ability to see success, plan for obstacles, and perform under pressure.

Whether you're preparing for a presentation, a game, a performance, or any other challenge, this combination of visualization, journaling, and celebrating progress creates an upward spiral of improvement. Each element reinforces the others, building a foundation of confidence that grows stronger with every practice session.

TRY IT: Create Your Own Vision Board

Dedicating some time and energy to this exercise can provide a massive boost to your motivation and confidence.

Here's how to get started:

1) Choose Your Space: Decide on a location where you'll display your vision board. Perhaps your desk, bedroom wall, or even the inside of your locker. This should be a place where you'll see it regularly.

2) Gather Your Supplies: You'll need a physical board or surface to work with, along with magazines, printouts, stickers, markers, and any other visual materials that speak to your goals and dreams.

3) Reflect on Your Aspirations: Take some time to get clear on what you want to achieve — both in the short-term and long-term. Consider areas like academics, extracurriculars, relationships, personal growth, and your vision for the future.

4) Create Your Board: Arrange your chosen images, words, and symbols on the board in a way that feels inspiring and meaningful to you. Don't overthink the layout. Let your intuition guide you.

5) Display Your Vision Board: Once you've created your masterpiece, hang it up in your designated space. Make sure it's somewhere you'll see it often so it can work its magic on your subconscious mind.

6) Maintain and Update: Your vision board isn't a one-and-done project. Revisit it regularly, adding new elements or rearranging things as your goals and priorities evolve.

As you create and interact with your vision board, pay attention to how it makes you feel. Visualize yourself achieving the things represented on the board. Let it fill you with excitement, determination, and a deep sense of purpose.

Remember, a vision board is a powerful tool, but it only works when combined with consistent effort and action. Use it to keep your focus sharp and your motivation high as you work towards turning your dreams into reality.

Chapter 7
Cultivating Curiosity and Lifelong Learning

The biggest risk is not taking any risk.
–Mark Zuckerberg

The Curious Case of Two Teenagers

It was a crisp autumn afternoon when the school bell rang, signaling the end of another day. As students flooded the bustling hallways, two teenagers, Nora and Lucas, made their way towards the exit, their paths destined to diverge in the years ahead.

On the surface, Nora and Lucas appeared quite similar. Both were bright, capable students navigating the vibrant chaos of high school. But scratch beneath the surface, and you'd uncover a striking contrast between them.

Nora was a perpetual questioner, her mind alive with curiosity. While her classmates were content to simply recite facts and formulas, Nora yearned to understand the "*why*" and "*how*" behind everything.

Rather than seeing school as a chore, Nora viewed it as a thrilling expedition, each subject a portal into uncharted realms waiting to be explored. On weekends, you'd find her tinkering with code, experimenting in the kitchen, or losing herself in thick volumes about the farthest reaches of the universe. For Nora, learning wasn't a means to an end - *it was a passion.*

Lucas, on the other hand, was the quintessential "*good student*". He dutifully completed his assignments, studied for tests, and checked all the boxes. But his approach lacked the spark that animated Nora's every step. Where she saw possibility, he saw only obligation. Where she had unquenchable curiosity, his motivation was simply to *"get good grades."* As the years passed, Nora and Lucas's paths couldn't have been more different.

Lucas stuck to his original plan. Good grades in college. A safe job. No risks. No unexpected turns. He thought having a steady plan meant success.

Nora's curiosity took her somewhere else entirely.

During a college internship, she discovered a community in rural Guatemala struggling with unreliable electricity. Instead of just feeling bad, she asked questions. How could solar technology help? What obstacles were preventing access? Her curiosity wasn't just academic — it was practical.

By graduation, Nora had partnered with local engineers to design a low-cost solar panel specifically for rural communities. Her "*what if*" approach had turned a classroom idea into a real solution that could change lives.

When Lucas heard about her project, he was stunned. How did she go from a random college internship to creating actual technology? The answer was simple: she never stopped asking questions. Never stopped wondering. Never accepted "*that's just how things are*" as a final answer.

While Lucas was working a predictable marketing job, Nora was traveling, speaking at conferences, and continuing to solve real-world problems. Her curiosity hadn't just opened doors — it had created entirely new pathways.

Nora saw the world as a series of fascinating puzzles waiting to be solved. Lucas saw the world as a set of instructions to follow.

What made the difference for Nora?

Curiosity

Your Secret Weapon for Growth

Curiosity isn't just a natural instinct; it's your innate superpower that unlocks endless opportunities for personal growth and self-discovery. As a teen, embracing curiosity is like having a magic key that opens doors to new ideas, experiences, and possibilities.

Why Curiosity Matters

Imagine navigating life with a magnifying glass, always ready to examine the world more closely. That's the essence of curiosity – a powerful force that pushes you to explore the unknown, challenge assumptions, and see things from fresh perspectives.

The Benefits of Being Curious

By asking questions, exploring new ideas, and challenging assumptions, you open yourself up to a world of growth and discovery. Curiosity fuels resilience, empowers you to adapt to life's challenges, and ignites personal evolution. Let's dive into some of the key benefits of cultivating a curious mindset.

Explore New Ideas: Asking "*why*" is the first step to mind-expanding discoveries. Curiosity compels you to dig beneath the surface, unraveling the fascinating reasons behind everything from historical events to cutting-edge scientific breakthroughs. It's like being an intrepid explorer, venturing into uncharted intellectual territory.

Challenge Assumptions: Curiosity is the antidote to accepting things at face value. It encourages you to question the status quo, consider alternative viewpoints, and arrive at well-reasoned conclusions. When you're curious, you're not afraid to ask probing questions and challenge conventional wisdom.

Adapt and Overcome: Life is full of ups and downs, but curiosity is your secret weapon for resilience. By seeking out new approaches and innovative solutions, you develop the adaptability to bounce back from setbacks and navigate challenges with confidence.

Fuel Personal Growth: Curiosity is the spark that ignites personal evolution. As you explore subjects in depth, you expand your horizons, broaden your perspective, and transform the way you engage with the world around you. It's not just about acquiring knowledge; it's about becoming a more well-rounded, open-minded version of yourself.

Make Informed Choices: Curiosity is the foundation of critical thinking. By seeking out diverse perspectives, analyzing data, and reasoning through complex issues, you develop the skills to make decisions based on sound judgment rather than blindly following the crowd.

Transform Your Social Life: Curiosity is the ultimate social lubricant. When you show genuine interest in others' stories and experiences, you forge more profound, more meaningful connections. Your openness and willingness to learn from diverse perspectives will draw people to you like a magnet.

The Magic of Conversation: Curious people make the best conversationalists. By actively listening and engaging in thought-provoking discussions, you create a space for ideas to flourish and relationships to thrive. You'll be amazed at the insights and shared interests that emerge when you approach conversations with an open, inquisitive mindset.

Your teenage years are a time of self-discovery, and curiosity is your compass. As you explore new hobbies, dive into fascinating books, and engage in stimulating discussions, each experience becomes a brush stroke in the masterpiece of your identity. Embrace the journey and let your curiosity lead the way.

Exploring New Interests and Hobbies

Hobbies are more than just pastimes; they're gateways to new passions, hidden talents, and a lifelong love of learning. In a world that can feel like an endless cycle of academic pressure and social expectations, hobbies provide a much-needed escape – a chance to lose yourself in something you genuinely enjoy.

Stress-Busting Hobbies

Being a teenager can be stressful. Between exams, extracurriculars, and the ever-shifting landscape of social dynamics, it's easy to feel overwhelmed. But here's the good news: nothing keeps stress at bay like engaging in hobbies that are near and dear to your heart.

You know the calm that washes over you as you lose yourself in the flow of a favorite activity – whether it's the rhythmic strokes of a paintbrush, the satisfying click of knitting needles, or the exhilarating rush of mastering a new skateboard trick. As you immerse yourself in these pursuits, your body releases a cascade of feel-good chemicals that melt away tension and promote a sense of well-being.

But the benefits of hobbies go beyond just momentary stress relief. When you carve out time for activities that truly light you up inside, you create space in your life for joy, self-expression, and personal fulfillment. Hobbies become a sanctuary where you can recharge your batteries and approach life's challenges with renewed energy and perspective.

Discover Hidden Talents

One of the most thrilling aspects of trying new hobbies is the opportunity to uncover talents you never knew you had. By stepping outside your comfort zone and embracing new experiences, you embark on a journey of self-discovery that can be deeply transformative.

Perhaps you'll find that you have a natural gift for capturing emotions through photography, or an uncanny ability to bring characters to life on the page. Maybe you'll discover a hidden aptitude for woodworking, or a knack for whipping up culinary creations that make your friends' taste buds sing.

As you explore different hobbies, you'll develop a rich tapestry of skills and experiences that make you a more well-rounded, adaptable individual. And who knows – you may even stumble upon a passion that could one day blossom into a fulfilling career path.

Find Your Tribe

Navigating the social landscape of teenage life can be daunting, but hobbies provide a natural way to connect with like-minded peers. When you join a club, team, or class centered around a shared interest, you instantly tap into a community of people who get you.

Picture the camaraderie that comes from working towards a common goal with your robotics team, or the deep discussions that arise during a book club meeting. These shared experiences create a bond that goes beyond the superficial, fostering friendships built on mutual understanding and respect.

And the best part? The connections you make through your hobbies often have a way of extending beyond the confines of the activity itself. You may find that the teammates who sweat alongside you on the field become your biggest cheerleaders in life, or that the friends you make in art class become your trusted confidantes.

So don't be afraid to put yourself out there and try something new. You never know who you might meet or what doors might open as a result.

Resources That Feed Curiosity

In a world that's constantly evolving, lifelong learning is the key to staying ahead of the curve. And the good news is that you don't need a classroom to keep expanding your mind. With a wealth of resources at your fingertips, you can embark on a journey of continuous discovery from anywhere, at any time.

Online Learning: A World of Possibilities

Welcome to the digital age, where the power to learn is quite literally at your fingertips. With platforms like Coursera, edX, and Udemy, you have access to an endless array of courses, tutorials, and educational content spanning every subject imaginable.

Want to learn how to code your own mobile app? There's a course for that. Curious about the intricacies of Ancient Egyptian history? You can dive deep into the topic with interactive lessons taught by world-renowned experts. The beauty of online learning is that you can tailor your education to your unique interests and goals, all at your own pace.

But online learning is about more than just convenience. Many platforms offer immersive, hands-on experiences that rival traditional classroom settings. Through virtual labs, real-world projects, and collaborative forums, you can develop practical skills and connect with a global community of learners who share your passions.

Books and Podcasts: Portable Inspiration

In a world of flashy digital distractions, there's something uniquely powerful about the timeless mediums of books and podcasts. With a good book or a thought-provoking podcast, you can transport yourself to new worlds, explore groundbreaking ideas, and gain wisdom from some of the most brilliant minds of our time.

Imagine immersing yourself in a memoir that chronicles a remarkable journey of resilience, or losing yourself in a science fiction novel that challenges your assumptions about the nature of reality. Through the written word, you can travel to the far reaches of human experience and imagination, all from the comfort of your favorite reading nook.

And when you're on the go, podcasts offer a portable dose of inspiration and enlightenment. Whether you're tuning into a history podcast that brings the past to life, or a science show that explores the cutting edge of discovery, you can transform your commute or workout into a mind-expanding adventure.

Community Learning: Strength in Numbers

While online resources and solitary pursuits have their place, there's something uniquely powerful about learning in a community setting. When you join a workshop, attend a seminar, or participate in a group project, you tap into the collective energy and wisdom of your peers.

Imagine the rush of collaborating with a team of like-minded individuals to bring a creative vision to life, or the thrill of engaging in a lively debate about a complex philosophical question. In these moments, you not only expand your knowledge and skills, but also learn from the diverse perspectives and experiences of those around you.

And the benefits of community learning extend far beyond the realm of academics. Through shared experiences and challenges, you develop crucial life skills like communication, collaboration, and empathy. You learn how to navigate different personalities, resolve conflicts, and work towards common goals – all skills that will serve you well in any future endeavor.

So, seek out opportunities to learn and grow alongside others. Join a study group, volunteer for a community project, or attend a local workshop. You never know what insights you might gain or what lifelong connections you might make.

The beauty of lifelong learning is that it's an ever-evolving journey. As you grow and change, so too will your interests and pursuits. Embrace the twists and turns, the challenges and the triumphs. Above all, never stop asking questions, seeking answers, and exploring the boundless possibilities of the world around you.

Because in the end, the most valuable education is the one that never stops – the one that keeps you curious, engaged, and forever reaching for new heights.

TRY IT: Curiosity Challenge

This chapter has emphasized the power of curiosity and the importance of embracing lifelong learning. Now, it's time to put those principles into practice.

Your challenge is to engage in three different exploratory activities that will broaden your horizons and nurture your natural inquisitiveness:

1) Explore a New Online Course: Visit a platform like Udemy and find a subject or skill that sparks your interest, but you haven't had the chance to explore. Select a course and commit to completing at least a few modules. Reflect on how it challenges your existing knowledge and pushes you to think in new ways.

2) Discover New Music: Step outside your usual music preferences and seek out artists, genres, or styles that you're unfamiliar with. Notice how the new sounds make you feel and what they reveal about the limits of your current musical knowledge.

3) Read a Book Outside Your Comfort Zone: Browse your local library or bookstore and select a title that takes you beyond your typical reading habits, whether it's a memoir, work of non-fiction, or a novel set in an unfamiliar culture or time period. Pay attention to how this new literary experience challenges your assumptions or broadens your understanding of the world.

After engaging in these three exploratory activities, take some time to reflect on your experiences in your journal. Consider what new passions or areas of interest you uncovered, how these explorations stretched your thinking, and how they might shape your future goals.

Chapter 8
The Art of Decision-Making

"The risk of a wrong decision is preferable to the terror of indecision."
— Maimonides

You're standing at a crossroads. In one direction lies the safe, familiar path you've walked a hundred times before. In the other, an uncharted trail winds its way into the unknown, full of uncertainty... *and potential.*

Which do you choose?

This moment of hesitation — of weighing your options and overthinking the potential outcomes — is one you'll face countless times throughout your life. Decisions, big and small, shape the very fabric of your world, whether you're deciding which extracurricular activity to join, which friendship to nurture, or how to spend a lazy Saturday afternoon.

The thing about these decisions is that they're rarely clear-cut. Sure, some choices are simple enough. Pizza or tacos. Netflix or YouTube. But the decisions that truly matter? Those are messy. They challenge you to think deeply, confront your fears, and even put your core values to the test.

Decision-making is a skill. One that can be learned, practiced, and honed over time. You don't need to have all the answers right away. What you do need is a reliable framework for making choices that not only reflect your deepest values, but also help you grow as a person.

In this chapter, we're going to explore that framework in-depth, arming you with the tools and strategies to navigate life's crossroads with confidence, wisdom, and an unwavering commitment to designing the future you desire.

The Weight of Every Choice

Choosing what to have for lunch isn't likely to alter the course of your life. However, many of the smaller choices we make on a daily basis can add up to something much bigger than we might initially realize.

The takeaway here is that it's not just the big, *"life-altering"* decisions that shape the trajectory of our lives. It's the small, everyday choices we make that quietly build the foundation for who we ultimately become.

Let's take this a step further...

The Butterfly Effect of Small Decisions

Have you ever heard of the concept of the *"butterfly effect"*? It's the idea that tiny, seemingly insignificant actions can set off a chain reaction, leading to massive, far-reaching outcomes. In the context of decision-making, this principle is everything.

Let's say, for example, that you decide to spend just 10 minutes a day practicing a new skill, like photography or coding. On its own, that might not seem like much. But over the course of a year, those daily 10-minute sessions add up to over 60 hours of dedicated practice. That's enough time to transform a casual interest into a genuine, marketable skill set.

On the flip side, small negative choices — like skipping one too many workouts or zoning out during class — can also snowball in ways that profoundly impact our lives. By recognizing the power inherent in these seemingly insignificant decisions, we can take proactive control of the narrative, understanding that each small choice is, in essence, a vote for the kind of person we're becoming.

Imagine a scenario where you decide to start meditating for just 5 minutes each morning. At first, it might feel like a tiny, almost negligible habit. But over time, that daily practice of mindfulness and self-reflection could have a profound impact, helping you manage stress more effectively, cultivate greater self-awareness, and make more thoughtful choices throughout your day. Those 5 minutes can quite literally reshape the trajectory of your life.

By being mindful of the butterfly effect at play in our decision-making, we empower ourselves to make choices that align with our values and long-term aspirations, rather than simply falling victim to the momentum of our habitual behaviors.

Why Decisions Feel So Overwhelming

If the idea of making decisions fills you with a sense of dread or paralysis, take comfort in the fact that you're not alone. There are several common reasons why decision-making can feel so overwhelming:

Fear of Regret: No one wants to make the wrong choice and be haunted by a lifetime of *"what-ifs."* The specter of regret can be paralyzing, even when the stakes feel relatively low. We tend to agonize over potential mistakes, convinced that any misstep will haunt us forever.

Too Many Options: Ever tried to pick a movie to watch from an endless streaming menu? It's exhausting, right? When presented with an abundance of possibilities, it's easy to get stuck in a loop of indecision, unable to determine the best path forward.

Pressure to Be Perfect: Society often makes it seem like every choice we make carries the weight of the world. But the reality is that life isn't a straight, perfect line. No single decision is going to define you forever. The pressure to make the *"right"* choice can be crippling, causing us to overthink and second-guess ourselves.

The good news is that you don't have to fear the decision-making process. Every choice you make, whether it ultimately works out or not, offers valuable lessons about yourself and your goals. The key is to approach each crossroads with an open, growth-oriented mindset.

The Foundation of Decision-Making

Before tackling any major life decision, it's essential to have a solid foundation in place. This means taking the time to know yourself honestly — your core values, your current priorities, and your long-term vision for the future.

Clarifying Your Core Values

Your values are like a personal compass, guiding you toward decisions that align with the kind of person you want to be. Take some time for deep reflection, and ask yourself:

- What do I care about most in life?

- What motivates me to keep going, even in the face of challenges?
- Whose qualities and achievements do I most admire, and why?

Your answers might reveal that you place a high value on creativity, kindness, adventure, or personal growth. Once you've identified your core values, decision-making becomes less about "*what's right or wrong*" and more about "*what feels most true to who I am.*"

Values provide an anchor — a stable point of reference that can ground you when the path ahead feels uncertain. Imagine you're trying to decide between pursuing a lucrative but unfulfilling career or taking a risk on a creative passion project. If one of your core values is "*making a positive impact,*" the choice suddenly becomes clear — <u>even if it's the more challenging path</u>.

Understanding Your Priorities

Every decision we make involves some degree of trade-off. You simply can't do everything at once, so it's crucial to have a clear sense of what matters most to you in the present moment. Perhaps academics are your top priority this semester, or maybe you're focused on cultivating deeper friendships and relationships.

Try ranking your current priorities like this:

1. School and learning
2. Family and personal relationships
3. Exploring hobbies and interests

When you know what's most important, it becomes easier to say "*yes*" to things that support your goals — and "*no*" to things that don't quite align.

Imagine you're debating whether to join the school's student council or participate in a community service club. If your priority is building stronger friendships right now, the service club might be the better fit, as it would allow you to engage with your peers in a meaningful way.

Prioritizing doesn't mean permanently relegating certain aspects of your life to the back burner. It's about being intentional and discerning with how you allocate your time and energy in the present so that you can continue to grow and evolve in the future.

Techniques for Smart Decision-Making

Now that you've laid the groundwork by clarifying your values and priorities, let's explore some practical strategies for navigating life's crossroads.

Weigh the Pros and Cons

When your mind is spinning with all the possible options, grab a pen and paper and make a simple pro-con list. Seeing the trade-offs of each choice laid out in front of you can provide much-needed clarity.

For example, imagine you're trying to decide whether to join the school newspaper. Your pros and cons might look something like this:

Pros:

- Build valuable writing skills
- Meet new people and expand your social network
- Add an impressive extracurricular to your college applications

Cons:

- Less free time and personal flexibility
- Potential stress during busy exam periods

Once you see the complete picture, the best path forward often becomes much more evident. The decision might still be a bit uncomfortable to make — *which is completely normal* — but this technique allows you to thoughtfully examine each option, rather than relying on gut instinct or emotion alone.

Tap Into Trusted Advice

While the ultimate decision is yours to make, seeking input from people you trust can provide an incredibly valuable outside perspective. A teacher, for instance, might offer insights you hadn't considered, or a close friend might remind you of personal strengths you may have overlooked.

The key is to use this advice as a guide, but not to let others decide for you. Their role is to provide an outside viewpoint, not to tell you what to do. Trust your gut instinct to make the final call.

Tapping into a support network can be particularly helpful when you're feeling stuck or uncertain. Talking through your thought process with someone you respect can often reveal hidden biases or assumptions you weren't even aware of. Their fresh perspective may illuminate new angles you hadn't considered.

Short-Term vs. Long-Term Thinking

Sometimes, what feels good or convenient at the moment isn't actually what's best for your long-term well-being. Let's say you're trying to decide whether to skip studying for an upcoming math test in order to go out with friends. Sure, the evening of fun might be enjoyable, *but how will you feel when the test rolls around and you're woefully unprepared?*

To navigate these types of dilemmas, ask yourself:

- How will I feel about this choice tomorrow?
- Next week?
- A year from now?

Thinking through the long-term effects can help you make decisions that genuinely align with your priorities and values.

This long-term mindset is crucial, as it prevents us from getting caught up in the lure of instant gratification. It allows us to step back, look at the bigger picture, and choose paths that may be more challenging in the short term, but ultimately serve us better in the long run.

Learning From Every Choice

Not every decision you make is going to lead to success. It's a fact. It's just the way it is. Some will feel more like missteps or setbacks — but those moments are just as valuable as the "*wins*" in your life.

Reframing Mistakes as Lessons

When a choice doesn't pan out the way you'd hoped, it's natural to experience feelings of disappointment or self-doubt. But rather than spiraling, try to reframe the experience in a more constructive light.

Ask yourself:

- What did this teach me about myself?
- What will I do differently next time a similar situation arises?
- How can I apply this newfound knowledge to future decisions?

<u>Remember, mistakes aren't failures</u> — they're stepping stones on the path to greater self-knowledge and resilience. Each *"misstep"* brings you one step closer to understanding yourself and how to navigate life's challenges more effectively.

Reframing setbacks in this way empowers you to view them not as dead-ends, but as opportunities for growth. The lessons you glean from these experiences can inform and strengthen your decision-making prowess, making you more equipped to handle whatever comes next.

Celebrating Your Courage

It's important to remember that making decisions, especially difficult or uncertain ones, requires a significant amount of bravery. So whenever you summon the courage to choose a path, take a moment to acknowledge and celebrate that achievement. You stepped up and took charge of your life, and that's something worth honoring, *even if the outcome wasn't perfect.*

Too often, we're quick to beat ourselves up over decisions that didn't work out as planned. But recognizing the inherent courage it takes to make a choice, regardless of the result, is a powerful act of self-compassion. It reinforces the idea that you are willing to take risks, learn from your experiences, and continuously grow as a person.

Avoiding Decision-Making Traps

As you navigate the decision-making process, be mindful of a few common pitfalls to avoid:

Analysis Paralysis: Overthinking a situation can leave you stuck in a loop of indecision. Remember, no decision is set in stone. You can always adjust course if needed. The key is to take action, even if it's a small first step.

Letting Fear Win: It's normal to feel scared or uncertain when faced with a difficult choice. But don't let those feelings of fear hold you back. Trust that you have the resilience to handle whatever comes next.

Following the Crowd: Just because *"everyone else is doing it"* doesn't mean a particular path is right for you. Make choices that authentically reflect your own values and priorities, not those of your peers.

The Right Choice

The antidote to these decision-making traps is to stay grounded in self-awareness and trust your internal compass. When you find yourself getting stuck in analysis paralysis, for example, take a step back and ask what your core values are telling you. If fear is holding you back, summon the courage to move forward anyway, knowing that you have the strength to adapt to whatever lies ahead.

The Power of Taking Ownership

When you take ownership of your decisions — both the successes and the setbacks — you step into a profound sense of personal power. Each choice becomes an opportunity to learn, grow, and actively shape the life you want to live.

So, don't wait for perfect clarity or certainty. Trust yourself, take a deep breath, and move forward with confidence. The future is yours to design.

The Adventure of Choosing

Decision-making isn't about always getting it right or making the "perfect" choice. It's about having the courage to choose, the humility to learn from your experiences, and the determination to keep moving forward, even in the face of challenges.

The path ahead may wind and twist in unexpected ways, but that's all part of the adventure. Embrace the journey, my friend. You've got this.

Along the way, remember to celebrate your victories, no matter how small. Acknowledge the bravery it takes to make tough choices. And when setbacks arise, as they inevitably will, reframe them as opportunities to grow stronger, wiser, and more resilient.

Your life is not a straight line, *nor should it be!* It's a vibrant, ever-evolving tapestry, with each decision you make contributing a unique thread to the overall design. Trust the process, lean on your values and priorities, and enjoy the adventure of charting your own course.

The world is waiting for the remarkable person you are becoming. So go forth, make your mark, and never stop exploring the endless possibilities that lie before you.

TRY IT: Your Decision-Making Roadmap

Every decision shapes the path you're walking. Whether it's big or small, having a clear plan can help you navigate with confidence. Let's turn what you've learned into a practical tool that makes decision-making less stressful and more intentional. Follow these steps to create your personal Decision-Making Roadmap and take charge of your future.

1) Identify Your Values

Write down 3-5 things that matter most to you, like kindness, creativity, or growth. These are your compass points to guide every decision.

2) List Your Priorities

What's most important to you right now? Rank your top 3 priorities—school, friendships, hobbies, or anything else. Knowing your focus makes decisions simpler.

3) Pick Your Tools

Choose 1-2 strategies from the chapter that works best for you, like making a pros-and-cons list or talking to someone you trust. Decide when and how you'll use them.

4) Learn From Mistakes

Write down one question to ask yourself when things don't go as planned, like: "What can I do differently next time?" This keeps mistakes from holding you back.

Reflection:

Every decision you make is a step toward the future you're creating. Your roadmap is a reminder that you have the tools to navigate life's twists and turns with confidence.

Chapter 9
Developing Emotional Intelligence

"Self-awareness is the foundation upon which we build the house of our lives."
— Rasheed Ogunlaru

You've already learned the power of curiosity, the importance of embracing challenges, and the transformative nature of lifelong learning. But what if I told you there was one more essential ingredient for unlocking your full potential?

The final piece of the puzzle is something called **emotional intelligence.**

In simple terms, emotional intelligence is the ability to understand, manage, and communicate your emotions in healthy, productive ways. It's about getting in tune with your emotions and using that self-awareness to make wiser choices in your relationships and everyday life.

Imagine a scenario where you're having an off day. The stress from a tough class, the lingering family drama, and the ever-shifting social dynamics of high school have all come to a head. And then, in a moment of frustration, you snap at your best friend over something trivial. The hurt and confusion in their eyes leave you feeling guilty and unsure of how to make amends.

But what if, in that charged moment, you had the presence of mind to pause and reflect on your emotions?

You might have realized that the overwhelming anxiety and irritability bubbling within you were the true culprits, *not your friend*. With a little self-awareness, you could have expressed your feelings openly: *"I'm so sorry, I've just been really stressed out lately and it's making me short-tempered. I didn't mean to take it out on you."*

This ability to navigate your inner landscape is the hallmark of emotional intelligence — and it's the key to unlocking your growth mindset in every facet of your life. When you can understand your own emotions and empathize with those around you, you gain the resilience to tackle challenges head-on, the flexibility to adapt to change, and the social skills to build meaningful connections.

The 4 Pillars of Emotional Intelligence

I'm sure you've encountered people in your life who seem to be at the complete mercy of their emotions. Maybe it's the classmate who flies off the handle at the slightest provocation, or the family member who spirals into a meltdown over the most minor inconvenience. Their emotions dictate their reactions, and they're unable to regain control or respond constructively.

Then, there are those individuals who seem to stay cool, calm, and collected, even in the most stressful situations. They're able to pause, reflect on their feelings, and make thoughtful decisions about how to proceed. What's the secret behind their composure? It all comes down to the four key pillars of emotional intelligence.

Pillar 1: Self-Awareness

First and foremost, we have self-awareness — the foundation upon which all emotional intelligence is built. This is your capacity to recognize your own emotions, understand how they shape your thoughts and behaviors, and develop a keen sense of your strengths, weaknesses, and triggers.

When you cultivate self-awareness, you gain the power to **pause**, reflect, and ask yourself:

"Okay, why am I feeling this way? What's the root cause of my anxiety/frustration/sadness?"

This moment of introspection gives you the ability to manage your emotions, rather than simply letting them control you.

Self-awareness is the key to unlocking your emotional intelligence.

When you can clearly identify the root causes of your feelings, you're empowered to make conscious choices about how to handle them. This foundation will serve as the bedrock for all the other pillars of emotional intelligence.

Pillar 2: Self-Regulation

Next up, we have self-regulation — the ability to navigate your inner landscape with intention and discipline. This is all about resisting impulses, controlling your reactions, and making conscious choices about how to respond to life's challenges.

Think of it like hitting the brakes when you feel a sudden rush of anger or frustration. Instead of lashing out, self-regulation allows you to take a step back, take a deep breath, and choose a more constructive path forward. Maybe you need to excuse yourself for a quick walk or journal about your feelings before re-engaging.

We've all encountered people who seem to operate on a hair trigger, exploding at the slightest provocation. They might start yelling, slamming doors, or making hurtful comments without a second thought. This lack of self-regulation can very quickly damage relationships and make it difficult for them to navigate challenges effectively.

But with practice, you can develop the discipline to control your impulses and respond in ways that serve you, rather than sabotaging your progress. Self-regulation is about finding balance and maintaining composure, even in the face of intense emotions.

Pillar 3: Motivation

Ah, motivation — the internal drive that propels you to pursue your goals and dreams. It's not just about chasing external rewards and accolades, but finding joy and fulfillment in the journey itself. When you cultivate this intrinsic motivation, you build remarkable resilience, allowing you to bounce back from setbacks and stay the course, no matter what obstacles arise.

We've all known someone who seems to give up at the first sign of difficulty, while others persevere through even the toughest challenges. The difference often lies in their motivation. The person with stronger emotional intelligence is driven by an internal desire to learn, grow, and improve rather than just seeking external validation or accolades.

Imagine you're working towards mastering a new skill, like playing an instrument or perfecting your coding abilities. The emotionally intelligent person finds genuine satisfaction in the process of improvement, celebrating each small victory along the way. Their intrinsic drive and belief in their potential will carry them through, allowing them to achieve their goal with a profound sense of accomplishment ultimately.

Pillar 4: Social Skills

Last but not least, we have social skills — your ticket to better communication, collaboration, and empathy. In a world where social dynamics can change in a flash, strong interpersonal abilities are essential. By actively listening, making eye contact, and showing genuine interest in others, you'll build trust, understanding, and the capacity for meaningful connection.

I'm sure you've experienced the difference between talking with someone who has excellent social skills versus someone who doesn't. The former makes communication feel effortless and enjoyable, while the latter can create tension, misunderstandings, and an overall unpleasant dynamic.

Emotionally intelligent individuals understand the importance of being attuned to others' needs and perspectives. They actively engage in conversations, pick up on social cues, and adapt their communication style to the situation at hand. This ability to connect with and empathize with those around them is a skill that can transform all of your relationships.

Emotional Intelligence and the Growth Mindset

As you've learned, emotional intelligence is the key to unlocking your full potential and navigating life's ups and downs. But what many people don't realize is how closely this skill is tied to the growth mindset principles we've explored throughout this book.

The hallmarks of emotional intelligence — self-awareness, self-regulation, motivation, and social skills — are all fundamental to cultivating a mindset focused on continuous improvement and resilience. When you develop these abilities, you gain the tools to tackle challenges head-on, adapt to change, and forge meaningful connections.

Think about it — a growth mindset is all about embracing setbacks as opportunities for growth rather than seeing them as fixed limitations. Emotional intelligence gives you the self-awareness to recognize when you're stuck in a negative spiral, the self-regulation to pause and respond constructively, and the motivation to persist through difficulties.

Similarly, being able to understand and empathize with the perspectives of others aligns perfectly with the growth mindset's emphasis on learning from diverse experiences and viewpoints. The more attuned you are to the thoughts and feelings of those around you, the better equipped you are to collaborate, communicate, and find creative solutions to complex problems.

In many ways, emotional intelligence and the growth mindset are two sides of the same coin. They're complementary skill sets that, when developed in tandem, allow you to approach life's challenges with a powerful combination of self-knowledge, resilience, and interpersonal finesse.

So, as you continue to nurture your emotional intelligence, see it as an extension of the growth mindset principles you've been honing throughout this journey. The more you can understand, manage, and communicate your emotions, the more you'll be able to unlock your true potential and become the adaptable, empowered individual you're meant to be.

With this foundation in place, let's now dive deeper into the key components of emotional intelligence, starting with the cornerstone of this essential life skill: *empathy*.

Empathy: The Cornerstone of Meaningful Connections

At its core, empathy is about stepping outside of our limited perspectives and striving to see the world through someone else's eyes. It's about cultivating the compassion and openness to truly listen, acknowledge, and validate the experiences of those around us. Empathy allows us to forge more profound, more meaningful connections, navigate conflicts with greater understanding, and cultivate a heightened awareness of the diversity that enriches our social landscape.

Let's dive into the core elements that make empathy such a powerful force:

Active Listening

Active listening is a fundamental aspect of empathy, crucial for clarifying misunderstandings and strengthening interpersonal bonds. Imagine being in a conversation where the other person continuously interrupts or seems distracted — it can feel incredibly frustrating and disconnected.

Active listening, on the other hand, involves giving your full attention, making eye contact, and responding appropriately to what the other person is saying. These small gestures, like putting away your phone or using verbal affirmations, show that you value the speaker's words and create a safe space for open dialogue.

By actively engaging in this way, we can better understand the feelings and perspectives of others, preventing conflicts that often arise from miscommunication. When someone feels truly heard and understood, they're more likely to reciprocate that sense of trust and connectedness, leading to more meaningful exchanges.

Perspective-Taking

Another vital component of empathy is perspective-taking - the ability to see the world through someone else's eyes and acknowledge their unique experiences and feelings. This practice helps reduce judgment and promote compassion.

For instance, if a friend seems distant or upset, instead of immediately assuming they're angry with you, try imagining what they might be going through. Are they stressed about an exam? Dealing with issues at home? Recognizing that everyone has their own battles can foster a more open and understanding approach.

Moreover, perspective-taking helps us appreciate diversity. As we learn to recognize that people think and feel differently based on their backgrounds, cultures, and personal histories, we enrich our worldview and become more adaptable communicators. We start to understand that our perceptions and opinions are not the only valid ones, opening us up to a richer, more nuanced understanding of the human experience.

Expressing Empathy

Putting empathy into action through words and gestures is pivotal for building trust, especially during conflicts. Simple actions like offering a comforting hug, listening patiently, or saying "*I'm here for you*" can have a significant impact on how others feel supported.

The key is to express empathy from a place of genuine care and understanding. During heated arguments, for example, acknowledging the other person's feelings can diffuse tension and pave the way for constructive dialogue.

This is important stuff, so let me give you some detailed examples of what this might sound like:

"*I can see how much this situation is affecting you. It's understandable to feel frustrated and hurt when you don't feel heard. I want you to know that your feelings are valid, and I'm here to listen and support you in any way I can.*"

"*I'm so sorry you're going through this tough time. It breaks my heart to see you in pain. Please know that you're not alone – I'm here for you, ready to listen or just sit with you in silence if that's what you need.*"

"*I can't imagine how overwhelming this must be for you right now. It's okay to feel lost and unsure. We'll figure this out together.*"

These empathetic expressions show that we're not just concerned with our own needs, but that we genuinely value the other person's perspective and emotional experience. This, in turn, helps create an environment where both parties feel heard and respected, making it much easier to find mutually satisfactory solutions.

Cultural Awareness

Empathy also requires cultural awareness, as every society has its norms and customs for communicating and expressing emotions. Being culturally sensitive means recognizing these differences and adjusting our behaviors accordingly.

For instance, maintaining eye contact is considered respectful in some cultures, while in others, it might be seen as confrontational. By understanding and respecting these nuances, we can interact more effectively with people from diverse backgrounds, enriching our social experiences and broadening our empathetic reach.

Cultural awareness also helps us appreciate the diversity of emotional expression. What may be considered an appropriate display of emotion in one culture could be seen as inappropriate or even disruptive in another. By recognizing and honoring these differences, we avoid making assumptions or judgments, and instead create an environment where everyone feels validated and understood.

Cultivating empathy is an ongoing journey of self-reflection and growth. By actively listening, considering different perspectives, expressing genuine care, and embracing cultural diversity, we can forge deeper, more meaningful connections with the people in our lives.

When we make a conscious effort to step into someone else's shoes, we unlock the ability to foster more compassionate, collaborative, and enriching interactions. Empathy has the power to bridge divides, resolve conflicts, and help us all feel a little less alone in this complex world. It's a skill worth cultivating, not just for our personal growth, but for the betterment of our communities and the world at large.

TRY IT: Empathy in Action

For this activity, you'll have the opportunity to put your empathy skills into action through a real-world interaction.

Identify a situation in your life where you can deliberately apply the principles of active listening, perspective-taking, and empathetic expression.

This could be anything from a conversation with a friend who's going through a difficult time, to a group project where you need to collaborate effectively with your peers. Whatever the context, your goal is to approach the interaction with heightened empathy and awareness.

1) Identify the Opportunity: Reflect on your daily life and relationships. Where do you see an opportunity to practice empathy? Perhaps it's a friend who has been more withdrawn lately, or a group assignment where tensions are running high. Choose a situation that feels meaningful and important to you.

2) Prepare Your Mindset: Before the interaction, take a few deep breaths and mentally prepare. Remind yourself to approach the situation with an open and curious mindset. Your goal is not to fix the other person's problems but to truly listen, understand, and validate their experience.

3) Engage with Empathy: During the interaction, pay close attention to the other person's verbal and nonverbal cues. Use techniques like reflective listening, validating their feelings, and offering empathetic statements.

4) Observe and Reflect: After the interaction, take time to reflect. How did the other person respond? What did you learn about their perspective? How might this have unfolded differently without your empathy skills?

5) Celebrate Your Growth: Recognizing your progress is essential. Acknowledge the empathy and emotional intelligence you demonstrated. Celebrate the meaningful step you've taken.

Empathy is a skill that takes practice, but the rewards are immeasurable. By engaging in this *"Empathy in Action"* activity, you're honing your abilities and making a positive impact on the people around you.

Chapter 10
Designing Your Future

"The best way to predict the future is to create it."
—Peter Drucker

Imagine standing at the edge of a vast, open landscape. It's your future, stretching out in every direction. But here's the twist: there are no paths, no roads, no signs. Instead, every step you take carves out a new trail, shaping where you go next. It's exhilarating. It's overwhelming, and most importantly — *it's yours to design.*

This isn't just a metaphor. *It's reality.* Your future isn't something that just happens to you. It's something you actively create through choices, actions, and the mindset you bring to every moment.

But how do you start?

How do you design a future that feels aligned with who you are?

That's what this chapter is about. We'll break the process into six actionable steps. Each one helps you move from dreaming about possibilities to building a life you're proud of.

As you dive into these steps, you might notice some familiar ideas from earlier chapters. That's no accident—it's intentional! These key concepts are trusted tools in your growth mindset toolkit, and revisiting them will strengthen your foundation. With this groundwork in place, it's time to look ahead and start shaping the future you've been working toward.

Let's begin.

Step 1: Discover What Drives You

Every meaningful journey begins with a sense of direction. But finding that direction requires understanding what truly matters to you — your values, passions, and unique vision for the life you want to live.

Why Values Are Your Compass

Think of values as your internal compass. They guide your decisions, helping you prioritize what's important and filter out distractions. When your actions align with your values, life is meaningful and fulfilling. When they don't, even success can feel hollow and pointless.

For example, if you value creativity but spend all your time following rigid routines, you might feel stifled. Conversely, if you value making a difference but focus on goals that feel self-serving, you might struggle to find motivation.

The trick lies in understanding your core values so that you can use them to help guide your path forward.

Discovering Your Core Values

To uncover your values, start by asking yourself these questions:

- What inspires me? Think about moments when you felt most alive or connected.
- What frustrates me? Sometimes, what you dislike in the world reveals what you care about changing.
- What do I admire in others? Consider the qualities you respect and want to emulate.

Let's say you admire honesty, creativity, and kindness. These become touchstones for your decisions. Whenever you're faced with a choice, ask: *Does this align with my values?*

Step 2: Define Your Vision

Once you've identified your core values, it's time to create a compelling vision for your future. This isn't about predicting every detail, but rather about gaining clarity on the kind of life you want to create.

Creating a Vision That Excites You

To begin crafting your vision, find a quiet space where you can reflect without interruption. Close your eyes and allow your imagination to run free, picturing your ideal future in as much detail as possible.

- Where are you living?
- What are you doing with your time?
- Who are the people in your life?

As you visualize your ideal future, don't hold back. This is your chance to dream big and imagine a life that genuinely excites you.

Maybe you see yourself:

- Launching a successful YouTube channel that showcases your passions and creativity
- Traveling the world, learning about different cultures, and making new friends
- Developing a groundbreaking app that makes a positive impact on people's lives
- Pursuing a fulfilling career in a field you love, like music, art, or science

Once you have a clear mental picture, write it down in vivid detail. Use sensory language to describe what you see, hear, and feel in your envisioned future.

As you reflect on your vision, ask yourself:

- How does this vision align with my core values?
- What parts of this vision feel most exciting, inspiring, or meaningful?

For example, let's say your vision includes becoming a successful YouTuber. If you value creativity, community, and self-expression, you might envision:

"I see myself creating engaging, inspiring content that resonates with a diverse global audience. My channel is a vibrant hub of creativity and connection, where I collaborate with other passionate creators and engage in meaningful discussions with my subscribers. Through my videos, I'm able to express my unique voice, share my talents, and make a positive impact on people's lives. My work is both challenging and fulfilling, allowing me to continuously grow, learn, and push the boundaries of what's possible."

Anchoring Your Vision in Reality

While dreaming big is essential, it's also important to identify concrete steps you can take to bridge the gap between where you are now and where you want to be.

Continuing with the example above, you might begin by:

- Researching popular channels in your niche and analyzing what makes them successful
- Developing your unique voice and on-camera presence through practice and feedback
- Learning key skills like video editing, scriptwriting, and SEO
- Networking with other creators and collaborating on projects
- Creating a consistent posting schedule and engaging with your audience regularly

By breaking your larger vision down into manageable steps, you make it feel more attainable. Each small action you take builds momentum, propelling you forward on the path to your ideal future.

Remember, your vision can evolve as you grow and learn. Stay connected to the core of what you want to create, and use it as a guiding light to navigate your journey.

Here is the expanded version with a word count of 919:

Step 3: Set the Right Goals

Dreams without action are just wishes. Goals are the bridge between where you are now and where you want to be. They turn your vision into concrete, achievable milestones that you can work towards every day.

Moving Beyond SMART Goals

In a previous chapter, we explored the SMART framework for goal setting — Specific, Measurable, Achievable, Relevant, and Time-bound. While this is a great starting point, designing a future that truly aligns with your values and aspirations requires going a bit deeper, or even being willing to bend and flex along the way.

Consider these additional layers when crafting your goals:

Flexible Goals: Life is unpredictable, and your priorities may shift over time. Build flexibility into your goals so you can adapt as needed without losing sight of your overall vision. This might mean setting a range instead of a fixed target *("I want to save $500-$1000 per month" instead of "I will save exactly $750 per* *month")* or building in regular checkpoints to reassess and adjust your goals as needed.

Process-Oriented Goals: While it's essential to have a clear end-result in mind, focusing solely on the outcome can be daunting and demotivating. Instead, try setting process-oriented goals that prioritize the habits and actions that will get you there. For example, instead of saying, *"I want to write a novel,"* set a goal to write 500 words every day. By focusing on the process, you build momentum and make progress more manageable.

Meaningful Milestones: Big, audacious goals are exciting, but they can also feel overwhelming. Break them down into smaller, manageable milestones that you can celebrate along the way. Let's say your ultimate goal is to launch your own podcast. Start by setting incremental goals like:

1. Research equipment options and choose a microphone
2. Brainstorm a list of 20 potential episode topics
3. Write scripts for your first three episodes
4. Record and edit a short practice episode
5. Design your podcast cover art and create a website

By focusing on these bite-sized steps, you turn a daunting project into a series of achievable tasks. Each milestone you hit builds momentum and confidence, propelling you forward towards your larger goal.

Aligned with Values: As you set goals, make sure they align with your core values and the vision you created in the previous step. Ask yourself, *"Does this goal move me closer to the life I want to create? Is it aligned with what matters most to me?"* If a goal feels out of sync with your values, consider how you can reframe it or find an alternative path that feels more authentic.

Remember, goal-setting is not a one-time event, but an ongoing process. Regularly review and reassess your goals to make sure they're still relevant and aligned with your vision. Celebrate your progress along the way, and don't be afraid to adjust your course as needed. The path to your dreams is rarely a straight line, but with clear, flexible goals as your guide, you'll stay motivated and on track.

Step 4: Build Systems for Progress

Goals give you a destination, but systems are the vehicle that gets you there. In other words, goals are the *"what"* and systems are the *"how."* Without reliable systems in place, even the best intentions can stall out.

The Science of Habits

At the core of any effective system are habits — the small, consistent actions you take on a daily or weekly basis. Your brain is wired to automate repetitive tasks, turning them into habits that require less conscious effort over time. When you repeat an action often enough, it becomes automatic, freeing up mental energy for more significant, more complex decisions.

For example, if you build a habit of reviewing your goals every Sunday evening, staying focused and on track becomes second nature. You no longer have to expend willpower or motivation to keep your goals front and center; it simply becomes a part of your routine.

Designing Systems That Work

To create systems that support your goals, start by identifying the daily or weekly habits that will move you closer to your desired outcome. If you're working towards better physical health, your system might include meal prepping on Sundays, going for a run every morning before school, and attending a yoga class twice a week.

Next, create cues or triggers that remind you to perform these habits. One effective strategy is to pair a new habit with an existing routine. Want to build a journaling habit? Try doing it immediately after brushing your teeth each night. By linking your new habit to an established one, you make it easier to remember and follow through.

Finally, track your progress and celebrate your wins along the way. Use a simple checklist, habit tracker, or app to record your daily actions. Seeing your consistency build over time can be a powerful motivator to keep going, even when you don't feel like it. And when you reach a milestone or achieve a goal, take time to acknowledge and celebrate your hard work. Positive reinforcement helps cement new habits and keeps you motivated for the journey ahead.

Step 5: Visualize Your Success

We've talked about this previously, but its importance rings especially true for designing your ideal future. Visualization is a powerful tool for keeping your goals front and center and priming your brain for success. By vividly imagining yourself achieving your goals, you engage the same neural pathways that are activated when you actually perform an action. In other words, visualization is like a mental rehearsal that prepares you to handle challenges, recognize opportunities, and perform at your best.

The Power of Mental Rehearsal

Elite athletes have long used visualization to improve their performance. Before a big race, a sprinter might close their eyes and imagine every aspect of their performance, from the moment they settle into the starting blocks to the feeling of crossing the finish line victorious. This mental rehearsal helps build confidence, reduce anxiety, and program the mind and body for success.

You can apply this same principle to your own goals. Let's say you have a big class presentation coming up. In the days leading up to it, take a few minutes each day to close your eyes and vividly imagine yourself delivering the presentation with confidence and ease. Picture yourself speaking clearly, engaging your audience, and fielding questions with poise. The more detailed and immersive your visualization, the more powerful its impact will be.

Creating a Vision Board

Again, you're already aware of this particular tool, but its value in helping you design your future cannot be overstated. A vision board is a collage of images, quotes, and symbols that represent what you want to achieve. It can include pictures of your dream college, inspiring quotes about perseverance, or a photo of someone who embodies the qualities you want to develop.

The key is to make your vision board as specific and meaningful to you as possible. Choose images and words that evoke a strong emotional response and make you feel excited and motivated when you look at them. Place your vision board somewhere you'll see it every day, like your bedroom wall or your locker at school. By keeping your goals and dreams visually front and center, you prime your subconscious mind to look for opportunities and take actions that move you closer to your desired future.

Visualization and vision boards are powerful tools for keeping your motivation high and your focus sharp. By regularly taking time to imagine your success and surround yourself with reminders of your goals, you train your mind to stay positive, proactive, and resilient in the face of challenges. So dream big, imagine vividly, and watch as your vision begins to manifest in reality.

Wyatt's Journey: How He Designed His Future

Meet Wyatt, a sixteen-year-old with a fascination for the ocean. From a young age, he's been captivated by marine life, spending weekends glued to nature documentaries and doodling whales and dolphins in his notebooks. His favorite place in town? The local aquarium, where he'd spend hours marveling at the shimmering jellyfish and the mesmerizing movements of stingrays.

Wyatt's dream? To become a marine biologist. But for a long time, that dream felt like a distant, unreachable goal. That is, until he decided to follow a structured plan like the one outlined in this chapter. Here is how he applied the teachings of this chapter to design his future.

Discovering His Values

Wyatt started by identifying what mattered most to him. He reflected on his love for discovery, his passion for nature, and his deep care for protecting the environment. These values pointed him toward a career where he could explore and contribute to preserving marine ecosystems.

He jotted down his core values in his notebook: *curiosity, environmental stewardship, and learning.* These became his guiding principles as he began crafting a plan for his future.

Defining His Vision

With his values in mind, Wyatt envisioned his future. He pictured himself working on a research vessel, diving into the depths of the ocean to study coral reefs, and contributing to conservation efforts for endangered species. He wrote down a clear statement:

"I want to be a marine biologist who helps protect ocean ecosystems and educates others about the importance of marine life."

He also started thinking about the small, immediate steps he could take to begin his journey.

Setting a Goal

Wyatt set an actionable goal to kickstart his path:

"By the end of this year, I will volunteer at the local aquarium and take an online course in marine biology basics."

The aquarium had always been his favorite spot in town, so he reached out to their volunteer coordinator, explaining his passion for marine life and his desire to learn. To his excitement, they welcomed him onto their team to help with guest tours and assist in the care of the smaller exhibits.

Building a System

To stay on track, Wyatt built a system that fit into his busy high school schedule. He volunteered at the aquarium every Saturday morning, where he shared his enthusiasm with visitors by leading discussions about marine ecosystems. During the week, he set aside Tuesday and Thursday evenings to work on an online course about marine biology, watching lectures and completing quizzes on topics like oceanic ecosystems and animal behavior.

He used a planner to track his schedule and even created a checklist to measure his progress—finishing one module in his course for every two weeks of volunteering. Seeing those checkmarks accumulate kept him motivated.

Visualizing Success

Each night before bed, Wyatt spent a few quiet minutes picturing his future. He imagined himself scuba diving alongside colorful schools of fish, recording data on shark migrations, and presenting his findings at scientific conferences. He also visualized smaller victories, like feeling confident explaining ocean conservation to aquarium visitors or acing a quiz in his online course. These vivid mental rehearsals kept his excitement alive and helped him stay focused on his path.

Wyatt even created a vision board above his desk, filled with photos of coral reefs, inspiring quotes from marine biologists, and even a postcard from the aquarium's gift shop that read: *"Protect What You Love."*

Cultivating Resilience

Of course, Wyatt faced setbacks along the way. On his first day volunteering at the aquarium, he accidentally spilled a bucket of water while cleaning a tank, earning some teasing from the staff. He felt embarrassed and out of place. But instead of letting that moment discourage him, Wyatt reminded himself that every expert starts as a beginner.

He journaled about the experience, reflecting on what he could learn. *"I'll ask more questions next time,"* he wrote. *"And I'll double-check everything before moving a tank!"* Slowly but surely, he gained confidence, and the staff began to trust him with more responsibilities, like preparing food for the aquarium's sea turtles.

When his online course got tough—especially the module on ocean chemistry— Wyatt pushed through by breaking the material into smaller sections and dedicating extra time to study. He leaned on his systems and his vision to keep him motivated.

By the end of the year, Wyatt had completed his online course, gained hands-on experience at the aquarium, and even received a glowing recommendation letter from the volunteer coordinator. But more importantly, Wyatt felt a new sense of confidence in his ability to pursue his dream.

Wyatt's hard work paid off. Not only did he make progress toward his long-term dream, but he also discovered how much he loved sharing his passion for marine life with others — a skill he knew would serve him well in his future career.

What about you?

What's your big dream?

Follow the steps in this chapter to design your ideal future and start making small and consistent steps toward your goal. I assure you that you'll be shocked by how quickly you can make measurable progress toward your ideal future.

TRY IT: Your Future-Planning Blueprint

Follow these steps to create your personalized blueprint:

Step 1: Identify Your Core Values

Write down 3–5 values that matter most to you. Think about what inspires you, what frustrates you, and the qualities you admire in others.

Example: *Creativity, helping others, curiosity.*

Step 2: Envision Your Ideal Future

Take five minutes to imagine your dream life. Where are you? What are you doing? Who's with you? Write a short paragraph describing this vision in as much detail as possible.

Example: *"I'm running a wildlife sanctuary, caring for animals, and educating people about conservation."*

Step 3: Set One Actionable Goal

Choose one small, specific step that aligns with your vision. Make sure it's achievable in the next 1–3 months.

Example: *"Volunteer at a local animal shelter on weekends."*

Step 4: Build a System

Create a simple routine to support your goal. Include when and how often you'll take action.

Example: *"Spend Saturday mornings volunteering and Wednesday afternoons researching animal care."*

Step 5: Visualize Success

Close your eyes and imagine yourself achieving your goal. What does it feel like? What steps got you there? Write a sentence or two describing this moment.

Example: *"I see myself at the shelter, confidently helping care for the animals and learning new skills."*

Step 6: Plan for Setbacks

List one or two challenges you might face and how you'll overcome them.

Example: *"If I feel nervous about volunteering, I'll remind myself that everyone starts somewhere and ask lots of questions to learn."*

Reflection

After completing these steps, take a moment to reflect:

- What excites you most about your plan?
- What's one thing you can do today to move closer to your goal?

Keep this blueprint somewhere visible, like your desk or journal, and revisit it often. Every small action adds up, bringing you closer to the future you're designing!

Chapter 11
Maintaining Momentum

> "Don't Watch the Clock; Do What It Does. Keep Going."
> — Sam Levenson

You and your best friend decide to hike up the local mountain. You're pumped. The sun is shining, the air is crisp, and the views? Incredible. But about halfway up, your legs start burning. Your once-perfect rhythm slows, and suddenly the summit feels ridiculously far away. Meanwhile, your friend is bounding ahead like a mountain goat, grinning ear to ear.

"*Come on!*" they yell. "*We're so close!*"

For a moment, you wonder, *"Why am I even doing this?"* The climb feels endless, and your motivation tanks. That's when your friend doubles back, pats you on the shoulder, and says, "It's *not just about the peak — it's about the climb. Look around!*"

And they're right. You pause, take in the view, and something shifts. The mountain hasn't gotten smaller, but your perspective has changed. You can do this.

Life's challenges are like that hike. Some days, you're fired up and unstoppable. Other days, you're dragging, wondering if the effort is even worth it.

Momentum — the energy that keeps you going — isn't something you find; *it's something you create*. It's a mix of strategy, self-awareness, and resilience that allows you to keep moving forward, even when the path is challenging.

This chapter is about how to maintain that momentum. You'll learn how to reflect on your goals, track your progress, and celebrate along the way. You'll also discover how to adapt when life throws you curveballs and how to keep your motivation alive during tough times. By the end, you'll have a clear toolkit to stay on track and enjoy the climb.

Are You Climbing the Right Mountain?

Here's a hard truth: Not every goal you set will stay relevant forever, *and that's okay!* The key is learning when to push forward and when to pivot.

Take a moment to reflect on your current goals.

Are they still lighting a fire in you?

Or are they starting to feel like obligations?

For instance, maybe you set a goal to ace your math class because you thought it would help you pursue engineering. But somewhere along the way, you realize your real passion lies in art. Does sticking with engineering still make sense?

Adjusting your goals isn't giving up; it's leveling up. It's saying, *"I've grown, and my priorities have grown with me."* Maybe the new goal is to apply to art school or start an independent design business. Whatever it is, don't be afraid to shift course if it means aligning your efforts with what truly inspires you.

Practical Tip: Schedule a regular *"goal check-in"* with yourself. Once a month, take 15 minutes to ask:

- Does this goal still excite me?
- Does it align with my values and long-term vision?
- What progress have I made, and what's holding me back?
- How can I adjust or refine this goal to better fit who I am now?

This habit keeps your goals fresh and relevant, ensuring you're climbing the right mountain. It also gives you the flexibility to adapt as your circumstances and passions evolve.

Turn Mountains Into Steps

Big dreams can feel overwhelming, like staring up at a massive peak with no trail in sight. The secret? Break it down into smaller, manageable steps.

Imagine you want to write a novel. Thinking about 300 pages can be paralyzing. But what if your first step was just outlining the plot? And the next was drafting one chapter? Suddenly, it feels doable.

Real-World Example: Remember Wyatt's dreams of becoming a marine biologist? His long-term goal feels massive: years of schooling, internships, and fieldwork. So, he breaks it down:

1. Volunteer at the local aquarium.
2. Take advanced biology in high school.
3. Research colleges with strong marine biology programs.
4. Apply for summer research internships.
5. Declare a marine biology major in college.

Every small step builds momentum and makes the more significant goal feel achievable. Plus, as Wyatt completes each milestone, he gains valuable experience and insights that inform the next phase of his journey.

Practical Tip: Write down your big goal and break it into 3–5 smaller milestones. Focus on completing one at a time. Each success will fuel your motivation to tackle the next.

Celebrate the Wins — Big and Small

Imagine playing a video game without checkpoints or bonus rounds. Boring, right? Goals are the same. Celebrating milestones keeps the journey exciting and reminds you of how far you've come.

When you hit a small win — like finishing a big homework assignment or running your first mile without stopping — take a moment to celebrate. High-five yourself, blast your favorite song, or treat yourself to something fun. These little victories are just as important as the big ones.

Why It Matters: Celebrations release dopamine, the feel-good chemical in your brain. This reinforces positive behavior, making you more likely to keep going. Recognizing your progress also gives you a sense of momentum and purpose, preventing you from getting discouraged.

Practical Tip: Create a reward system for your goals.

Small wins = small rewards (e.g., a favorite snack, an hour of free time).

Big wins = big rewards (e.g., a movie night, new gear for your hobby).

Set aside a dedicated "*celebration fund*" in your budget so you always have something to look forward to. These small acts of self-appreciation can make a big difference in sustaining your motivation.

Build a Scoreboard — Track Your Progress

Ever noticed how satisfying it is to check something off a to-do list? That's the power of tracking.

A scoreboard gives you a visual reminder of your progress. It could be as simple as a notebook, a habit-tracking app, or a whiteboard in your room. Seeing your progress keeps you motivated and accountable.

If your goal is to practice guitar every day, mark an "X" on your calendar for each day you practice. Watching those X's pile up creates a sense of achievement and builds momentum.

Practical Tip: Experiment with different tracking tools until you find one that works for you. Apps like Habitica or Notion are great for digital tracking, while journals or sticky notes are perfect for analog fans. The key is to find a system that feels intuitive and easy to maintain.

You can also get creative with how you display your progress. Some people like to color in a grid or add stickers to a wall calendar. Find a method that keeps you engaged and excited to mark your achievements.

Embrace Change

Life is unpredictable. New interests emerge, old passions fade, and external factors throw curveballs. Learning to adapt your goals is a crucial skill.

Take Jack, for example. He started high school with dreams of being a professional skateboarder. But after an injury and a newfound love for graphic design, his focus shifted. Instead of clinging to his original goal, Jack pivoted. He started designing skateboards and launched a small online shop, combining his love for skating and creativity.

Adjusting doesn't mean failure; it means growth. Sometimes, the path you envision at the start isn't the one that ultimately fulfills you. The key is remaining open to exploration and following the trail that lights you up.

Practical Tip: When you feel stuck or uninspired, ask yourself:

- Is this goal still aligned with who I am and what I value?

- What changes can I make to reignite my passion for this pursuit?
- Are there adjacent interests or skills I could explore that might be a better fit?

Avoid getting boxed in by your initial plan. Stay curious, experiment, and be willing to adjust course if it means getting closer to your true calling.

Stay Motivated During Tough Times

Even the most driven people hit slumps. The key to pushing through is having strategies to stay motivated.

Coping Strategies: When stress hits, try mindfulness techniques like deep breathing or journaling. For example, before a big test, take three deep breaths to calm your nerves and clear your mind. You can also try meditation, yoga, or simply going for a walk to reset.

Lean on Your Network: Surround yourself with people who lift you up. Whether it's a supportive friend, a teacher, or a family member, having someone to cheer you on makes all the difference. Share your struggles and let them encourage you.

Visualization: Picture yourself achieving your goal. Close your eyes and imagine crossing the finish line, hearing the applause, and feeling the rush of success. This mental rehearsal can keep you focused when the going gets tough.

Affirmations: Use positive self-talk to counter doubts. Say things like, *"I've got this,"* or *"Every step brings me closer to success."* Repeating these affirmations builds confidence and resilience.

Reframe Setbacks: When you hit a roadblock, avoid seeing it as a failure. Instead, view it as a chance to learn and grow. Ask yourself, *"What can I take away from this experience that will make me stronger?"*

Having a toolkit of coping strategies allows you to weather the storms and keep moving forward, even when motivation starts to wane.

Build Habits That Last

Success isn't just about bursts of motivation; it's about consistent habits that support long-term growth.

Start Small: Pick one habit that aligns with your goal and stick to it. For example, if you want to run a 5K, start by jogging for 5 minutes a day.

Track Consistency: Use a habit tracker to build streaks. Watching your progress over time keeps you committed.

Stay Flexible: If a habit stops working, tweak it. Life changes, and your routines should too. Experiment until you find what works best for you.

Expanding Your Mindset

As you work through the steps of designing your future, it's essential to keep an open, expansive mindset. Far too often, we unconsciously limit ourselves, constraining our dreams to what we think is "*realistic*" or "*attainable*." But the truth is, your future holds a world of limitless possibilities that extend far beyond your current circumstances.

When you take the time to deeply reflect on your values, passions, and greatest aspirations, you may find that your initial vision feels a bit... *small*.

Maybe you start by imagining yourself in a stable, respectable career, living a comfortable life. But as you dig deeper, you realize that what truly excites you is the prospect of starting your own business, or traveling the world as a digital nomad, or spearheading a social impact initiative that could change lives.

Don't be afraid to dream bigger. In fact, embracing a genuinely expansive vision is essential to designing a future that feels energizing, meaningful, and in alignment with your most profound sense of purpose. By consciously pushing the boundaries of what you think is possible, you open yourself up to opportunities and pathways you may have never considered before.

Of course, it's important to balance that expansiveness with practicality. You don't want to get so carried away by lofty visions that you lose sight of the concrete steps required to turn them into reality. But by cultivating an open, curious mindset, you can continue to refine and elevate your goals in ways that feel both exciting and achievable.

Fueling Your Journey with Curiosity

As you work through the process of designing your future, it's crucial to maintain a spirit of curious exploration. Rather than approaching this journey with a rigid, prescriptive mindset, stay open to discovery, adaptation, and ongoing evolution.

Curiosity is the driving force behind innovation, resilience, and personal growth. It's what compels you to ask questions, experiment with new approaches, and continuously seek out fresh perspectives. And in the context of designing your future, it's an essential quality to cultivate.

After all, the world is constantly changing, and the path from your current circumstances to your desired destination will inevitably be filled with surprises, obstacles, and unexpected opportunities. The more open you are to asking *"why?"* and *"how?"* — the better equipped you'll be to navigate those twists and turns.

Curiosity allows you to reframe challenges as intriguing puzzles to solve, rather than roadblocks to overcome. It sparks your creativity, fueling innovative solutions. And it keeps you attuned to signals and insights that could dramatically alter the trajectory of your plans.

By approaching this process with curiosity, you give yourself the freedom to adapt, refine, and improve upon your original plans. You don't get stuck in a single, rigid trajectory, but rather remain open to the insights and epiphanies that will undoubtedly arise along the way.

So, as you dive into the process of designing your future, make curiosity your constant companion. Celebrate the thrill of discovery. Embrace the lessons hidden within setbacks. And always, always keep your mind open to the possibility that your dreams may grow and transform in ways you never could have predicted.

After all, the future isn't static — it's a living, breathing entity, shaped by your choices, your actions, and the openness with which you approach each new chapter. By nurturing your curiosity, you ensure that the journey of designing your destiny remains an exciting, fulfilling, and constantly unfolding adventure.

Your Future Starts Now

By aligning your goals with your values, building systems that support your progress, and cultivating resilience, you have everything you need to design a life that feels meaningful and fulfilling.

Remember, this isn't a one-time process. Your vision will evolve, your goals will shift, and new opportunities will arise. The key is to stay curious, adaptable, and committed to growth.

So, take the first step today. Write down your values, set a goal, or start visualizing your success. The future is yours to design — one choice, one action, one moment at a time.

Final Thoughts

Momentum isn't about rushing to the finish line; it's about finding joy in the journey and staying committed to your path. By reflecting on your goals, celebrating your wins, and embracing change, you'll build the resilience to tackle any mountain — one step at a time.

Now, climb your mountain. You've got this.

Afterword

Look how far you've come.

Remember when you first opened this book? Whether you were drowning in self-doubt or already glimpsing your potential, that version of yourself feels a bit distant now, doesn't it?

That's because your mindset has transformed. Maybe a little — perhaps a lot — but either way, you are now equipped with the knowledge and tools to make incredible things happen in your life.

Through these pages, you've discovered profound truths that will forever change how you view yourself and your potential:

That setbacks aren't roadblocks — *they're launch pads.*

That challenges aren't threats — *they're invitations to grow.*

That your potential isn't fixed — *it's infinite.*

Think about what this means: You now possess something most people spend their entire lives searching for — **the power to actively shape your destiny**. This isn't just about positive thinking or wishful dreaming. It's about having concrete tools and strategies that transform obstacles into stepping stones toward your goals.

Afterword

Your growth mindset isn't just another self-help concept to be filed away and forgotten. It's a living, breathing companion that walks beside you, transforming each experience — *good or bad* — into wisdom that propels you forward. Every challenge you face, every setback you encounter, every victory you achieve becomes fuel for your continued evolution.

Picture yourself five years from now. See how much stronger, wiser, and more authentic you've become. That future isn't just a dream floating in the distance — *it's a vision that you've already begun building* — one decision, one action, one day at a time.

Your community, your mentors, your supporters — they're all essential characters in your story. Let them lift you up when the journey feels challenging. Let them witness your transformation and celebrate your victories. Let them be inspired by your courage to grow, to change, to become more than you ever thought possible.

So here you stand, at the threshold between who you were and who you're becoming. *The sleeping giant within you?* It's wide awake now, ready to take on whatever challenges lie ahead.

A future of endless possibility stretches out before you.

Make it extraordinary.

Bibliography

Bradley, J. (2023, July 10). *The role of accountability in personal growth and Transformation*. Medium. https://johnbradley1.medium.com/the-role-of-accountability-in-personal-growth-and-transformation-c54b73b66317

Ozbay, F., Johnson, D. C., Dimoulas, E., Morgan, C., Charney, D., & Southwick, S. (2007, May). *Social support and resilience to stress: From neurobiology to clinical practice*. Psychiatry (Edgmont). https://pmc.ncbi.nlm.nih.gov/articles/PMC2921311/

Suttie, J. (2017, November 13). *Four ways social support makes you more resilient*. Greater Good. https://greatergood.berkeley.edu/article/item/four_ways_social_support_makes_you_more_resilient

Ginsburg, K. (2018, September 4). *Support teens to release emotions*. Center for Parent and Teen Communication. https://parentandteen.com/support-teens-release-emotions/

Made in United States
North Haven, CT
10 February 2025

65624861R00065